HIKERS AND CLIMBERS GUIDE
TO THE SANDIAS

Donna D. Petty

HIKERS AND CLIMBERS GUIDE TO THE SANDIAS

Edited by Mike Hill

University of New Mexico Press
Albuquerque

© 1983 by Mike Hill.
All rights reserved.
Manufactured in the United States of America.
International Standard Book Number 0-8263-0648-9.
Library of Congress Catalog Card Number 82-19992.
Design: Barbara Jellow.
Second Edition. (First Edition published in 1977 by Adobe Press.)
Third paperbound printing, University of New Mexico Press, 1988

Library of Congress Cataloging in Publication Data
Main entry under title:

Hikers and climbers guide to the Sandias.

  Bibliography: p.
  Includes index.
  1. Hiking—New Mexico—Sandia Mountains—Guide-books.
2. Rock climbing—New Mexico—Sandia Mountains—Guide-
books.   3. Trails—New Mexico—Sandia Mountains—Guide
books.   4. Natural history—New Mexico—Sandia Mountains
—Guide-books.   5. Sandia Mountains (N.M.)—Description.
I. Hill, Mike, 1944–
GV199.42.N62S264   1983   917.89'61   82-19992
ISBN 0-8263-0648-9 (pbk.)

CONTENTS

PREFACE

This book was written to help hikers and climbers enjoy the Sandia Mountains. The intent is not necessarily to promote hiking and climbing in the Sandias, but to provide useful information for people who are already participating in these activities or are interested in trying them. It is my hope that the book will help diffuse and minimize visitor impact on the fragile environment of the Sandias. Hikers and climbers represent the ultimate hope for protecting the integrity of this unique wilderness sanctuary, and it is to them that the book is dedicated.

The first attempt at a hiking and climbing guidebook for the Sandias was *Guide to the Sandia Mountains* by Larry Kline, published in 1970, followed by the original version of this book in 1977. The present edition has been significantly revised and updated and is certainly the most comprehensive guidebook yet produced for the Sandias. It was written with the understanding that the primary market for the book would be hikers, and, although a sizable section on rock climbing is included, care has been taken to make the hiking section as comprehensive as possible. Also included in this edition is information on cross-country skiing and snowshoeing. I believe that the reader will find that each section of the book in some way complements the others.

It would be terribly remiss at this point not to acknowledge the contributions made by numerous members of the local hiking and climbing community to the publication of this book. I can hardly overstate the value of this group effort, including assistance provided by the Forest Service, but I hesitate to single out individuals for fear of neglecting anyone's contribution. I hope these individuals will find satisfaction in knowing that they have helped light the way for those who will follow in their footsteps.

GENERAL INFORMATION

The Sandia Mountains are part of a local uplift located south of the Rocky Mountains on the east slope of the Rio Grande trough. Situated immediately east of Albuquerque, the mountains reach a maximum elevation of 10,678 feet from a starting elevation of approximately 6,000 feet. *Sandia* is the Spanish word for watermelon. Perhaps the comparison of the mountains with a slice of watermelon is invited by the pink hue of the west face at sunset. Whatever the reason for their name, the Sandia Mountains have been neighbors to a succession of cultures, beginning with Paleo-Indian hunters, who arrived many thousands of years ago and hunted now extinct species of game. More recent Indian arrivals established permanent dwellings in the mountains, but our knowledge of them is also scarce. Recorded history in the Sandias began with the early Spanish, who provided the place names, but Spanish ranches, homesteads, and settlements are now part of history. Today, these ancient mountains, with their diverse flora, fauna, and geological formations, offer an escape from twentieth-century urban life. There is little doubt that the primary value of the Sandias is now recreational. Accordingly, in 1978, Congress included some 31,000 acres of the Sandias in the National Wilderness Preservation System. Now the mountain is yours to enjoy, and motorized vehicles are restricted.

Weather

The climate in the Sandias varies greatly with altitude. The temperature differential between Albuquerque and Sandia Crest can easily be 20°F or more. A drop of 3°F for every 1,000-foot increase in altitude is approximately standard. Hikers should carry along a sweater or jacket in the summer months and be prepared for afternoon thunderstorms. Winter temperatures rarely rise above freezing and a record low of -32°F has been recorded.

Cooling Power of Wind Expressed as "Equivalent Chill Temperature"
This chart shows the danger of freezing exposed flesh for properly clothed persons.

Wind Speed		Temperature (°Fahrenheit)																			
Calm	Calm	40	35	30	25	20	15	10	5	0	−5	−10	−15	−20	−25	−30	−35	−40	−45	−50	−55	−60
Knots	MPH	Equivalent Chill Temperature																			
3–6	5	35	30	−25	20	15	10	5	0	−5	−10	−15	−20	−25	−30	−35	−40	−45	−50	−55	−65	−70
7–10	10	30	20	15	10	5	0	−10	−15	−20	−25	−35	−40	−45	−50	−60	−65	−70	−75	−80	−90	−95
11–15	15	25	15	10	0	5	−10	−20	−25	−30	−40	−45	−50	−60	−65	−70	−80	−85	−90	−100	−105	−110
16–19	20	20	10	5	0	−10	−15	−25	−30	−35	−45	−50	−60	−65	−75	−80	−85	−95	−100	−110	−115	−120
20–23	25	15	10	0	−5	−15	−20	−30	−35	−45	−50	−60	−65	−75	−80	−90	−95	−105	−110	−120	−125	−135
24–28	30	10	5	0	−10	−20	−25	−30	−40	−50	−55	−65	−70	−80	−85	−95	−100	−110	−115	−125	−130	−140
29–32	35	10	5	−5	−10	−20	−30	−35	−40	−50	−60	−65	−75	−80	−90	−100	−105	−115	−120	−130	−135	−145
33–36	40	10	0	−5	−15	−20	−30	−35	−45	−55	−60	−70	−75	−85	−95	−100	−110	−115	−125	−130	−140	−150
WINDS ABOVE 40 HAVE LITTLE ADDITIONAL EFFECT		LITTLE DANGER			INCREASING DANGER (Flesh may freeze within 1 minute)				GREAT DANGER (Flesh may freeze within 30 seconds)												

Winter landscape. Photo by Carl Smith.

Cool weather and wind chill (see chart) cause effective low temperatures that are not to be trifled with. As in any mountainous area, the weather is unpredictable, and a certain amount of caution is advisable. Typically, the rainy months are July and August, but significant rain can fall during other months of the year, particularly in the autumn. The winter months almost always see snow, which generally exceeds 100 inches per year on the higher parts of the mountain. See Appendix A for an eleven-year summary of Sandia Crest weather data.

Plant Life

The earth is divided into seven climatic zones. Each zone has its own characteristic vegetation types. The climatic zones vary with both latitude and altitude. A 1,000-foot altitude increase is approximately equal to a 300-mile latitude increase in its effects on plant and animal distribution. In other words, one can move from one climatic zone to the next either by changing latitude or, as in the Sandias, by changing altitude. The climatic conditions on Sandia Crest are approximately the same as might be found at a lower altitude some 3,000 miles to the north along the coast of southern Alaska.

The Sandias encompass four climatic zones: the Upper Sonoran Zone at an approximate altitude of 5,000 to 7,000 feet, the Transition Zone at 7,000 to 8,000 feet, the Canadian Zone at 8,000 to 10,000 feet, and the Hudsonian Zone above 10,000 feet. The only climatic zones not found in the Sandias are the Tropical and Lower Sonoran zones on the low end of the scale and the Alpine Zone at the high end.

In the Upper Sonoran Zone, which exists up to about 7,000 feet in the Sandias, typical forms of plant life are various types of grasses and shrubs as well as box elders, cottonwoods, and a few willows at the lower elevations. Juniper and piñon trees are common to about 7,500 feet, along with some grey oak. The Transition Zone supports the ponderosa pine and the gambel oak, the latter found mostly on the east side. The Canadian Zone is populated by the aspen and douglas fir, with some white fir and Rocky Mountain maple. Here the trees are denser than in the towering ponderosa stands of the Transition Zone. The highest reaches of the Sandias are home to the corkbark fir, the Engelmann spruce, the douglas fir and the limber pine. In all, 13 varieties of coniferous trees are found in the Sandias along with the several broadleaf varieties.

Wildflowers are well represented in the Sandias.

Ponderosa pine in Del Agua Canyon. Photo by Mike Hill.

They bloom mostly from May through August with a few in April and September. Probably the rarest plants in the Sandias are five species of native orchids. Fifteen hundred species of plants can be found in the Sandias.

A combination of climatic change, mining, grazing, wildfire, and logging activities has significantly changed vegetation and affected distribution. In many areas these activities have altered the existing plant structure with pockets of oak, aspen, or grasses growing in place of the previous plant population.

The heaviest concentration of plant life is on the eastern slopes of the Sandias, where the best growing conditions exist. Along the crest itself, conditions are particularly harsh.

Wildlife

The Sandias are located within a wildlife refuge and are home to a large number of wild species. In all, there are 58 species of mammals, 34 species of reptiles, 6 species of amphibians, and 189 species of birds. Some of the more interesting mammals are mule deer, bighorn sheep, grey-tailed antelope, ground squirrel, bobcat, swift fox, gray fox, mountain lion, ringtailed cat, black bear, coyote, weasel, badger, and porcupine. Most of these animals, however, are very reclusive and rarely seen. Very common at all altitudes on the mountain are the squirrels and chipmunks. The largest of the birds in the Sandias are the golden eagle, the turkey, the turkey buzzard, the great horned owl, and various types of hawks. However, there are many other species to interest avid birdwatchers.

At least two species listed on the 1974 endangered species list have been sighted in the Sandia Mountains: the southern bald eagle and the American peregrine falcon. Among the other animals that once inhabited the Sandias but no longer exist there are the grizzly bear, the wolf, the pronghorn antelope, the elk, and the prairie dog. For those bird and animal species still present, the size of the mountain's habitat is decreasing at an alarming rate. Private developments close to the mountain and increased human impact on the mountain will ensure the continued decrease of wildlife in the Sandias.

Checklists have been compiled for wildlife in the Sandia Mountains. See appendices B, C, and D for checklists of birds, mammals, and reptiles/amphibians. A film on plants and animals of the west face of the Sandia Mountains, produced by Zane Dohner, is available through the New Mexico Wildlife Federation, the U.S. Forest Service, and the Albuquerque Public Schools.

Looking toward South Peak from lower Embudo Canyon. Photo by Mike Hill.

Geology

The Sandia Mountains were formed as a result of upward pressure within the earth's crust. They are a massive block of the earth's crust that tilted sideways because of a rupture along a north-south fault line roughly corresponding to the west face. The west face of the Sandias is the vertical face of this tilted block, and the gently sloping east side is the top surface of the block. The area of greatest faulting was probably located three to four miles west of the present crest ridge, and the total vertical displacement may have exceeded 26,000 feet. The west face offers the best view of the geological makeup of the Sandias because of the exposed cross-section of the great uplifted block.

At the top of the west face a veneer exists with thin

Looking north from the upper Tram Terminal area with limestone bands along the Crest Ridge in background. Photo by Mike Hill.

horizontal layers of light-colored rock. This rim of rock consists of alternating layers of shale and limestone which were formed from ocean sediments during the Pennsylvanian Age 250 to 300 million years ago. Other layers of sediments have weathered away exposing the Pennsylvanian Limestone layer which now forms the top surface of the east side of the Sandias. On the other side of the uplift fault to the west, the same limestone strata remain about 15,000 feet below the floor of the Rio Grande Valley. One can see these limestone strata and several characteristic types of fossils on the upper sections of the La Luz Trail. Sandwiched between the limestone rimrock and the granite below is the Great Unconformity: a 1,100-million-year gap in which no geological features were formed. Below the Great Unconformity is the ancient Precambrian granite formed 1,350 to

Blocks of weathered Precambrian granite in Embudo Canyon. Photo by Mike Hill.

1,400 million years ago as a result of cooling magma. The Sandia granite on the west face is a coarse aggregate composed primarily of quartz, feldspar, and mica. Limestone and sandstone with some granite in places where the limestone layer has been stripped away compose the top and east side of the mountain.

Map Availability

Topography of the Sandia Mountains is shown on three 7½-minute U.S. Geological Survey maps. The Placitas map shows the Sandias from the town of Placitas to about one mile north of Sandia Peak (North Peak). The Sandia Crest quad continues south past Sandia Crest almost to South Sandia Peak. The Tijeras quad covers the Sandias from South Sandia Peak down past

Tijeras Canyon. The maps are available either locally or from the U.S. Geological Survey Distribution Center in Denver, Colorado. While these maps are topographically correct, the trails are often shown incorrectly or not at all. The map accompanying this publication shows both hiking trails and topography in the Sandias. Several special-use maps are also available through the Forest Service.

HIKING IN THE SANDIAS

Man first set foot in the Sandia Mountains sometime in the early dawn of civilization. It would be fascinating to know when a human being first stood on Sandia Crest, and what he thought about the ancient spires of the west face and the Rio Grande Valley beyond. Those first prehistoric hikers have been followed by a succession of different races and cultures who have both used and enjoyed the forest resources.

The reasons for hiking the Sandias are as numerous as the people who have hiked them. Pragmatic pursuits such as hunting and wood gathering were probably an early reason, in addition to a desire for adventure, a love of nature, and a natural curiosity. These latter categories are of increasing importance in our leisure-oriented society. People need to get away, to explore the quiet majesty of the mountains, and to drink from a clear, unpolluted mountain stream. While these activities are increasing in popularity, the wilderness is con-

© 1981 Jonathan A. Meyers

stantly under attack in the name of progress. It is our obligation to help preserve that wilderness for future generations. Now, back to the subject of hiking! The following section provides the hiker with general information on hiking in the Sandia Mountains.

Weather

As previously mentioned, there is often a significant temperature variation with altitude. Most people are surprised at how much cooler the air is on Sandia Crest, particularly during the winter months. For hiking in the early morning or late afternoon, it is always advisable to carry along at least a jacket or sweater—any time of year. The wind along the crest ridge produces even lower effective temperatures.

A poncho or other raingear is usually useful during late summer or early fall. It frequently rains in the mountains while the valley is in sunshine. One special hazard of the rainy season is lightning. When a thunderstorm is imminent or in progress it is important to stay away from the crest ridge. Also avoid clearings and localized high spots.

During the winter be prepared for plenty of snow and cold weather. Hiking above 7,000 feet will often require snowshoes or tour skis, and above 9,000 feet it is usually precluded without this equipment.

Water

Water availability in the Sandias is partly a function of the season. Many small creeks and arroyos carry water during the spring meltoff or during rainy periods. The flow of water is greatly diminished during the dry months and the best place to obtain water is near a spring (marked on the topographical maps by the symbol ᴑᴧ). There are at least 26 springs in the Sandias, many of which are not marked on the standard topographic maps. As one would expect, springs are common in canyons and arroyos while ridges and high places are less likely to have water. Water flowing near its source should be unpolluted although I recommend water purification tablets as a reasonable precaution. Despite the possibility of obtaining water on the trail, hikers should carry water when starting out. Do not depend on finding water unless you are certain of its availability.

Elevation Gain

The total elevation gain from bottom to top of the Sandia Mountains is slightly less than 5,000 feet. Most

Bird's-eye view of the Sandias as seen from a hangglider. Photo by Paul Horak.

of the trails described in this section have less than a 3,000-foot elevation gain. While the average hiker travels up to three miles per hour on level ground, this figure drops significantly with increasing elevation. A gain of more than 500 feet per horizontal mile results in strenuous hiking. Average hiking time for this type of trail is closer to one or two miles per hour. Many of the trails in the Sandias have both flat and steep sections, however, so an overall average may be misleading.

Fire Restrictions

During especially dry months the Forest Service sometimes issues fire restrictions which prohibit smoking and campfires. This type of restriction would occur between April and July. If fire conditions are especially severe a full fire closure may be put into effect, prohibiting hikers and campers from the forest area altogether. If in doubt check with the Forest Service.

Footwear

Many trails in the Sandias cover granite or limestone rock that can be quite rugged. The best overall footwear is still a well-fitting pair of hiking boots with lug soles. Jogging shoes are increasingly popular and work very well when the trail is neither too rugged nor too muddy. Their most glaring weakness is lack of ankle support. Other acceptable footwear includes hunting boots, work boots, and military boots. Venture out in cowboy boots, sandals, and platform shoes at your own risk.

Clothing

Some of the clothing seen in the mountains appears to be more appropriate to bar-hopping than hiking. In the interest of function the following brief suggestions are offered:

Socks—Whatever works for you is fine. Most people prefer at least one thick pair of socks but not more than two thick pairs. Wool and synthetic blends are good; cotton is less desirable.

Pants—Pants should be comfortable and loose fitting. Wool is particularly good in cold weather. Shorts are comfortable in summer but be careful of sunburn.

Shirt—Any comfortable shirt is good for summer. Wool is preferred in winter because it continues to insulate when wet. Long underwear (polypropylene is best) will keep the wool off your skin.

Outerwear—In summer you will want a windbreaker and perhaps the additional insulation of a sweater or insulated vest. In winter it is important to keep from overheating. A system using wool shirt, sweater, and synthetic-filled vest allows you to adjust insulation. A shell parka keeps the wind and snow off. Save the down parka for rest stops and use a wool cap.

Accessories

A heavy backpack can spoil a hike that is otherwise enjoyable and memorable. While paring down your load, however, don't make your hike memorable by forgetting something that you'll need. Well-prepared hikers carry moleskin, toilet paper, water bottle, food, first aid kit, topo map, matches, sunglasses, sunscreen, flashlight, poncho, and a daypack to carry it all in. Leave the hatchet and portable radio at home.

Hypothermia

Hypothermia is the process by which a person is unable to maintain his normal body temperature owing to cooling of the body. The body temperature gradually drops and unless the trend is reversed, death may result. Also referred to as exposure, hypothermia is one of the leading causes of outdoor recreational fatalities. Hypothermia is particularly treacherous because it gradually decreases a person's ability to think clearly and logically which in turn makes it more difficult to take the necessary steps to remedy the situation. Hypothermia cases usually have at least three things in common: insufficient or inappropriate clothing for insulation, damp clothing usually from precipitation or overexertion, and failure to shield the body from the wind. Panic is often the other major contributor. Winter months are potentially the most critical, but hypothermia as a result of unpreparedness can also be a real danger during the rest of the year. Every hiker should become familiar with the causes, symptoms, prevention, and treatment of hypothermia. Hypothermia has been studied extensively and literature on the subject is available from a number of sources. An excellent publication on hypothermia is included in the bibliography at the end of this book. Please note also the publication dealing with frostbite. A further information source on hypothermia is a film entitled "By Nature's Rules," produced by the Safeco Insurance Co. and available through the Forest Service at 517 Gold S.W. in Albuquerque.

Winter Hiking

Winter hiking in the Sandias has never been as popular as summer hiking, primarily because winter travel demands a more knowledgeable and better-prepared hiker. Snowshoes or cross-country skis are usually required at the higher elevations, as well as specialized clothing and equipment. Weather is treacherous, hiking times are longer, and trails can be difficult to locate. In general, the mountains are less forgiving of mistakes in the winter. On the other hand, winter travel can be rewarding for the hiker who takes the time to prepare for it. Each season has its own unique charm, and the mountains are never more fascinating than in the snow. So go ahead and enjoy the mountains in the winter too, but before you start out, make sure you are well equipped and well informed and always inform someone where you are going and when you intend to return. Don't hike alone unless you are well aware of the possible consequences.

The La Luz Trail in winter. Photo by Alan Kennish.

Forest Service Tours

When possible, guided snowshoe hikes and cross-country ski tours are offered from January through March by the Forest Service; guided summer hikes are also offered. Call the Sandia Ranger Station for more information on these guided tours.

Camping

There are no designated overnight campgrounds in the Sandias; however, backpackers are permitted to camp overnight in nondesignated areas. When possible, choose a campsite that has been used before in order to avoid additional blackening from campfires, etc. Since you will need water, it is most convenient to camp downstream from a spring. There are many more springs than are shown on the topo maps, and nearly every major canyon has at least one spring that flows most of the year. If you are following a trail along the high ground, such as the Crest Trail, be prepared to carry water with you. Please read the section on fire restrictions and note that smoking and campfires are sometimes prohibited. Small campstoves are usually acceptable except during a rare full fire closure. Finally, you will occasionally notice a heap of trash that someone has left beside his former campsite. Please help eliminate this outrageous practice.

Dogs

Many hikers have been disappointed to find out that the household pet was unexpectedly short of endurance and tender of paw. More than one of these animals has had to be carried out by the master, testing the limits of friendship between man and his best friend. Start with a short hike if your dog is untested. Remember also that the dog will get thirsty on a hot day. If your dog might hassle the other hikers, keep him on a leash, and when he relieves himself on the trail, kindly remove the offending deposit from the trail.

Mountain Rescue

There are several search and rescue organizations which have been established to help locate and assist lost or injured hikers, and a number of people undoubtably owe their lives to the assistance provided by these groups. If a hiker is definitely overdue in returning, a responsible party can initiate a search-and-rescue effort by contacting the State Police. Prior information on pre-

cisely where the hiker intended to go as well as an estimated time of return would obviously aid the rescue
effort.

Literature

In addition to this book, information on the national
forests in general and the Sandias in particular is available in brochures from the Tijeras Forest Service Ranger
Station. Other publications of related interest are listed
in the bibliography.

Hiking Ethics

Please observe the following common-sense rules in
addition to those mentioned above:
 a. The Sandias are located within a wildlife refuge.
No firearms are permitted.
 b. Please do not drop litter or bury litter beside the
trail; pack it out with you. Introduce yourself to the
habit of helping pack out litter you find on the trail.
 c. Locate latrines away from trails and well away
from streams. Burn or bury your toilet paper and
bury accompanying waste.
 d. Don't cut across switchbacks in the trail. This
hastens erosion and usually does not save you any
time or energy.
 e. Don't cut live vegetation. It is also prohibited by
law to remove any trees, no matter how young, and
certain other types of vegetation from the national
forest.
 f. At least one hiker in the Sandias has been killed
by a rock thrown from above. Don't intentionally
roll rocks down slopes or throw rocks off cliffs.
 g. Please! No fireworks or spray paint.

TRAIL DESCRIPTIONS

The following trail descriptions are intended to provide information including:

A. Whether the trail is maintained by the Forest Service.

B. The approximate length.

C. The approximate elevation gain.

D. The availability of water.

E. How to find the trailhead.

F. A general description of the route.

Whether or not the trail is maintained does not necessarily indicate the quality of the trail, although the maintained trails are generally in better shape. A maintained trail is generally an official Forest Service trail; non-Forest Service trails are designated as unmaintained. As previously mentioned, water availability is often a function of the season. See the accompanying map for the relative location of the trails in the Sandias.

Piedra Lisa Spring Trail

Partially maintained. This trail is also called the Del Agua Spring Trail and has two trailheads. The south trailhead is near the Juan Tabo picnic area; the north trailhead is near the Piedra Lisa Spring, north of the Del Agua Canyon. The trail is maintained only from the Juan Tabo trailhead to the Rincon.

From the Juan Tabo trailhead it is two miles to the Rincon and about another four miles to Piedra Lisa Spring at the other end of the trail. Elevation gain is 1,200 feet from the Juan Tabo trailhead to the Rincon with a 2,000-foot drop in altitude from the Rincon to the Piedra Lisa trailhead. To reach the Juan Tabo trailhead, travel north past Juan Tabo picnic area for about 0.8 mile to a crude parking area south of the road. Park your car and walk north on a well worn trail past a Forest Service trail sign.

After 0.3 mile you will come to the intersection of Juan Tabo Canyon (also known as Juan Tabo Arroyo) and Waterfall Canyon. This point where the two streambeds intersect is one of the most significant trail intersections in the Sandias. The Fletcher Trail follows Juan Tabo Canyon upstream, the Waterfall Canyon Trail follows Waterfall Canyon upstream, the Movie Trail bears to the east up the ridge between the two canyons, and the Piedra Lisa Spring Trail heads north from the intersection toward the Rincon. Follow the trail as it continues winding on to the north until you crest the Rincon. The Rincon is the prominent ridge of small peaks that lies roughly east-west and is a continuation of the Shield. Past the Rincon the trail becomes less worn; however, the trail continues on over the Rincon and down the other side, crossing the south fork of Del Agua Canyon about one mile farther on. From the

The Knife Edge on the Shield in the foreground with the Needle in the background, as seen from the Piedra Lisa Spring Trail. Photo by Mike Hill.

south fork, the trail traverses northeast across a ridge and intersects the north fork of Del Agua Canyon one mile past the south-fork crossing. After crossing the north fork, the trail continues north to the right of a small peak, and enters Piedra Lisa Canyon. The trail then follows the canyon on its north side the rest of the way down past Piedra Lisa Spring and past the metal water tank, a short distance farther on, which marks the trailhead. In the lower part of the canyon you will notice the smooth granite rock ("Piedra Lisa" in Spanish) for which the spring is named. If you wish to hike the trail from north to south, reach the Piedra Lisa trailhead by traveling east from Interstate 25 on the Placitas road. After traveling three or four miles turn south on Forest Road No. 445 and continue for several miles until you come to a small jeep trail which leads east a short distance to the trailhead.

Rincon Spur Trail

Unmaintained. This trail is an offshoot of the Piedra Lisa Trail, which follows the Rincon east directly to the ridge of the Shield. Length is 0.5 to 0.8 miles. Elevation gain is 500 feet. The trail begins where the Piedra Lisa Trail crosses the ridgeline of the Rincon. It then follows the ridgeline toward the east, generally keeping to the north side of the ridge. The trail is not well worn and is difficult to follow but gradually works its way toward the ridge of the Shield. When you reach the base of this ridge, the trail ends, and one can either continue on up the ridge (see rock-climbing section) or scramble out along the huge shelf that crosses the lower part of the Shield. Caution: don't climb up anything that you can't safely retreat from.

Movie Trail

Unmaintained. Length is 1.5 miles from trailhead to the Prow (see rock-climbing section). Elevation gain is 1,400 feet. This trail was originally made for the motion picture *Lonely Are The Brave*. The trailhead and first 0.3 mile are the same as for the Piedra Lisa Spring Trail. At the Waterfall Canyon junction the Movie Trail veers off to the right and travels east up the north side of the canyon. The original trail, after a steep initial climb, ended less than half a mile from the streambed. At this point, the trail is broad and well worn. The trail continues, however, cutting north up the side of the ridge degenerating into a number of steep paths which converge again at the crest of the ridge. This ridge eventually helps form the south rim of Upper Juan Tabo Canyon and also runs directly into the northwest ridge of the Prow. The trail follows the ridgeline to the Prow.

A further extension of the trail skirts the Prow to the south and continues up loose rock to the Southeast Saddle. From this point it is then possible to continue on to the Needle.

Waterfall Canyon Trail

Unmaintained. This short trail leads to a 35-foot waterfall south of Juan Tabo Canyon. Length from the Waterfall Canyon-Juan Tabo Canyon intersection to the waterfall is 0.75 mile. Elevation gain is 700 feet. See the Piedra Lisa Spring Trail description to reach the intersection of Waterfall Canyon and Juan Tabo Canyon. The first streambed that you will cross while traveling north on the Piedra Lisa Spring trail leads out of Waterfall Canyon. Turn right at this point and follow Waterfall Canyon upstream on either side of the streambed. Some scrambling may be necessary to negotiate steep spots in the stream. The trail ends at the main waterfall which may be circumvented by climbing up from the north or south. The waterfall usually flows during the summer months. In winter it freezes, producing 20 to 40 feet of high-angle ice and providing a favorite practice climb for ice climbers.

Fletcher Trail

Unmaintained. This trail extends 1.5 miles from the Piedra Lisa Spring Trail to the ramp of the Shield, with a net elevation gain of 1,400 feet. The lower section of this trail, which has been rediscovered and cleared, is apparently part of an older trail, perhaps once used by sheepherders. It probably provides the quickest access to most of the Shield. The trail is, however, quite faint in places and rather difficult to locate from either end by a person

who has not been on it. The upper part of the trail above UNM Spire involves more difficult scrambling and is recommended only for experienced hikers.

Begin by hiking up the Piedra Lisa Spring Trail to the intersection of Juan Tabo Canyon and Waterfall Canyon. Continue up the streambed of Juan Tabo Canyon and lift out of the streambed onto the eastern bank 250 yards before the arroyo abruptly turns to the east. The trail parallels the arroyo around the inside of the turn, then crosses to the northern bank and continues up a steep ridge toward the Shield. Leaving the ridge, the trail turns to the south and follows an irregular contour around the hillside to the base of UNM Spire. From this point on, the hike becomes considerably more rugged. Staying immediately adjacent to the overhead cliffs, follow a large crack in the granite face upward from the southern base of UNM Spire to the ramp of the Shield. Hands are essential in negotiating the steep and partially exposed route along the crack, particularly at Dripping Springs where the rock is wet and slick. Fletcher Trail ends in the vicinity of a large, shallow cave located 75 feet above the ramp. Once again, don't get onto something that you can't safely get off of.

La Luz Trail

Maintained. This is the most popular trail for reaching the crest from the west side of the mountain. The present trail is the most recent of three La Luz trails that wind up the west face of the mountain and is the one described here. Total elevation gain from trailhead to Sandia Crest is 3,700 feet. Distance from trailhead to Sandia Crest is 7.0 miles; from the trailhead to the upper tram terminal is 7.8 miles. The trail is well marked and easy to follow in summer.

Hikers on the La Luz Trail.
Photo by Alan Kennish.

The trailhead is reached by driving north on Tramway Road past the tramway cutoff or east on Tramway Road from Interstate 25. Go north on the Juan Tabo turnoff and continue to the end of the paved road, turn to the right between the second set of stone pillars, toward the Juan Tabo picnic area. Drive past the picnic area to an upper-level parking lot that marks the trailhead. A Forest Service sign marks the beginning of the trail.

The first section of the trail is not particularly steep and you can make good time as the trail gradually traverses up toward La Cueva Canyon. At the one-mile point you will come to the Tramway Trail junction. This trail leads down past the La Cueva picnic area and on to the tramway. As you continue up, the small piñon and juniper trees are gradually replaced by larger species such as ponderosa pine. After about 2.5 to 3.0 miles, at a sharp bend in the trail, you will cross a stream marking the entrance to Chimney Canyon. If the weather is clear, you can see the radio towers standing at the head of the canyon just above and to the right of the towering walls of Muralla Grande.

A bit farther on, the Thumb comes into view off to the southeast. It appears as a large impressive pinnacle from this view. Farther on is La Cueva Canyon overlook, off to the right of the trail. It must be hiked up to but offers a spectacular view of the canyon below.

At this point the trail has entered upper La Cueva Canyon and continues to get more scenic with its many impressive rock walls and spires. Eventually, one passes a blackened, shallow cave and comes to a trail sign warning the hiker of further travel in winter.

At the warning sign the trail crosses to the south side of La Cueva Canyon and begins a long series of switchbacks up the large talus slopes that form the lower northeast base of the Thumb. This is the beginning of the most strenuous section of the trail; however, the beauty of the surroundings offsets the hard work.

The trail finally reaches a small saddle at the top of the talus slopes where it branches. One branch traverses north above the old La Luz mine (an old lead and silver mine which has been out of production since before the turn of the century) and ends directly south of the curio shop at the crest. This section of trail is quite steep but is the shortest way to reach the crest.

The south branch follows a more gentle incline along the limestone rim and ends at the upper tram terminal, a little over a mile farther on. For a strong hiker in a hurry, the La Luz Trail will take two and a half to three hours to travel from bottom to top and somewhat less from top to bottom. For a less hardened hiker or a more leisurely hike, allow as much as four to five hours for the trip up, and allow a full day to hike up the trail and return. Do not attempt the La Luz Trail in winter unless you are a well-equipped experienced hiker, and are familiar with the trail.

There is one significant variation in the above trail description worth mentioning for those who wish to cut out some of the monotonous switchbacks on the lower portion of the trail. At the fifth switchback up from the bottom of the La Luz Trail, a sign marks the Tramway Trail junction. If you follow the Tramway Trail for about 150 yards the trail will fork and you should take the left, or uphill, branch. You will then be on a steep and unmaintained path which makes its way up the south side of a ridge. You rejoin the La Luz Trail shortly after reaching the top of the ridge. The variant trail is rough, but the cross-canyon view of people plodding their way along the La Luz switchbacks eases the temporary discomfort.

CAUTION
Every summer a number of people become lost while hiking on the La Luz Trail. If at any time you are not walking on a very well-worn trail, you are NOT on the La Luz Trail. If you find yourself in this predicament, retrace your steps until you are certain you have returned to the trail.

In addition to the present La Luz Trail there were at least two older La Luz trails. The lower sections of these older trails roughly coincide with the upper section of Tramway Trail but begin at the road north of La Cueva picnic area. The older trails continue up the canyon from the La Luz-Tramway Trail junction and rejoin the present trail near the top of the ridge which the present trail ascends via a sizable number of broad switchbacks. The

Summit of the Frog in upper La Cueva Canyon, with the La Luz Trail in the background. Photo by Carl Smith.

Looking west toward the Chimney in upper Chimney Canyon. Photo by Mike Hill.

oldest trail then branches off to the left and ascends Chimney Canyon (see Chimney Canyon Trail). The other trail continues up La Cueva Canyon where the present trail branches. It then traverses north up the limestone band, past the old La Luz mine, and to the summit. This is the trail that is shown on the current (1972) Sandia Crest topo map.

Chimney Canyon Trail

Unmaintained. Length is approximately 2.5 miles. Elevation gain is 2,000 feet. Hiking time is 3 to 5 hours up and 2 to 3 hours down. The Chimney Canyon Trail was once the upper section of one of the old La Luz trails. It begins as an offshoot from the present La Luz Trail and ends at the radio towers north of the crest.

The trail starts at the entrance to Chimney Canyon

which is reached by hiking up from the bottom of the La Luz Trail. After hiking about 2.5 miles, you will cross a small stream at a sharp inside bend in the trail. Follow this stream into the canyon. Since there is no definite and continuous trail up the lower part of the canyon you must perform a certain amount of routefinding and will have two basic choices in starting the hike. The first, which is the most straightforward and arduous, is simply to follow the streambed and bushwhack your way up the canyon proper. You will soon find yourself enveloped in brush and deadfall and will probably wish you had taken this alternate route: at the La Luz Trail junction begin by hiking up a steep path which goes up the north side of the canyon from the streambed, passing to the left of some rock outcroppings. After a steep initial section the trail begins to level out and bears to the right as it cuts across the north side of the canyon until you reach open ponderosa slopes. As you continue to make your way through the ponderosa you will be gradually forced into the narrow upper part of the canyon. At this point you should begin to see the Chimney, a slender pinnacle of granite at the head of the canyon.

Continue toward the Chimney and skirt to the north of its base until you reach the point where further progress in the same direction becomes relatively impossible. You will then find yourself at the base of a steep couloir to your left just north of the Chimney, and it is here that the real scrambling begins. Climb to the top of this couloir (watch for loose rock) and continue north up the hillside and across the small aspen meadow. At the other side of the aspen meadow you should pick up a reasonably well-worn trail which switchbacks up through the limestone band and exits at the radio towers. To locate the trailhead at the top, drive north from the crest past the radio towers to the last cluster of buildings. The trail starts down just west of these buildings. Water is usually available at a spring about halfway down the canyon.

Nearly every type of thornbush known to man seems to be located in Chimney Canyon. Unless you have masochistic tendencies, don't do this hike in shorts.

Tramway Trail

Partially maintained. Length is 2.2 miles. This trail begins in the vicinity of the lower tram terminal and continues north, traversing the foothills and finally skirting around a ridge to join the La Luz Trail. The upper end of the trail is clearly marked. The junction occurs near the lower end of the La Luz Trail at the fifth switchback from the bottom and is identified by a Forest Service sign. The lower trailhead for the Tramway Trail is vague because of construction that has obliterated things near the lower tram terminal. Total elevation gain for the trail is 500 feet and hiking time is ¾ to 1½ hours each way. Reach the lower tram terminal by traveling north on Tramway Road then east to the Sandia Peak Tram Co. See the La Luz Trail description for access to the upper trailhead.

La Cueva Trail

Maintained. Length is .25 mile. This trail begins at the La Cueva picnic area and travels due east ending at the intersection with Tramway Trail. Elevation gain is negligible. Reach the La Cueva picnic area by taking the Juan Tabo picnic area exit off Tramway Road, then veering to the right on Forest Service Road No. 3333B (a dirt road a short distance beyond the cattle guard). During the summer you can drive all the way to the picnic area.

During part of the year it is necessary to start hiking at a road block a short distance below the picnic area.

As an alternative, instead of branching off onto Tramway Trail, the hiker can continue east into lower La Cueva Canyon. Any one of a number of faint trails into this scenic canyon make a very enjoyable day hike.

Elena Gallegos Land Grant

One of the choice areas of the Sandia Mountains is a block of land formerly known as the Elena Gallegos Land Grant. This land is located on the west slope of the mountain and encompasses the entire Bear Canyon area and part of Domingo Baca Canyon as well. As private land, this area was off limits to hikers. However, pending completion of a complicated land swap, approximately 7,000 acres, including the mountainous portion of the land grant, are to come under the jurisdiction of the forest service and will be added to the wilderness area.

As this book goes to press, no trail system worth mentioning exists in the higher elevations of the Elena Gallegos grant although the forest service is sure to establish trails in due time. In the meantime, the area will offer plenty of new off-trail hiking. To learn the status of hiking trails in the Elena Gallegos grant area, I would suggest contacting John Southwick or some other knowledgeable person at the forest service ranger station in Tijeras.

Embudito Trail

Maintained. Length is 5.6 miles from trailhead to the Crest Trail junction. The total elevation gain from the trailhead to Deer Pass is 3,200 feet. The trail is reached by following Montgomery Blvd. east almost to its end and then turning north on Glenwood Hills. Follow this street until it ends at a fence with a set of wooden steps continuing over the top of the fence. The hike starts at this point and goes north, then east along a dirt road which passes to the south of a large concrete water tank, and gradually leads down into the arroyo bed. About 0.3 miles past the water tank the canyon takes a sharp turn to the south, and the broad arroyo suddenly narrows as the canyon becomes more sharply defined. Although a trail follows the stream on up the canyon, the main trail continues east up a hillside and ends up on the north side of the canyon 100 to 200 feet above the stream bed. The trail is well worn and easy to follow. If you follow the stream too far, you can locate the trail by cutting directly north up the side of the canyon.

About 1.4 miles past the water tank the trail crosses the canyon and continues up the south side of the canyon. The altitude gain begins to become more pronounced during this section. At the 3.0-mile point, about half a mile up the canyon from the crossing, are the remains of a crude shelter. Water is usually present from a nearby spring. At the 4.2-mile point, you reach the Three Gun Spring Trail junction at Oso Pass. Deer Pass is slightly over a mile farther up the trail and the Crest Trail junction is just 0.2 mile farther on. South Peak is best reached by working your way north along the crestline from Deer Pass. The South Peak area is one of the most enchanting parts of the mountain, and well worth the hike.

Embudo Trail

Unmaintained. Length is approximately three miles from trailhead at the mouth of Embudo Canyon to the junction with Three Gun Spring Trail. Elevation gain is

Partially frozen waterfall in upper Embudo Canyon. Photo by Mike Hill.

1,300 feet to Three Gun Spring Trail and an additional 680 feet to Oso Pass (see description for Three Gun Spring Trail). If the hiker continues all the way to Deer Pass, the total elevation gain is 2,900 feet and the total distance involved is about six miles each way.

At this writing there is residential construction activity in the vicinity east of Tramway Road necessitating a generalized description for reaching the trailhead. Travel east on either Menaul Boulevard or Indian School Road as far as possible. From Menaul bear south or from Indian School bear north and onto a series of dirt roads which seem to head into the obvious major canyon to the east. The dirt roads will lead into an arroyo you follow to the large concrete flood control dam. At this point you will start walking, following the arroyo up for about a mile until the canyon narrows at a small concrete waterfall just below a spring. As the canyon narrows you will pick up a well-worn trail which generally follows the center of the canyon. As one travels east the canyon gradually widens out and after about 0.8 mile the trail, which is now faint, veers north and follows the main arroyo. At this point there are two choices. The first alternative is to traverse up the ridge to the east. The low point in the ridge just below the prominent peak is called Post Pass. After gaining the ridge, continue north along the faint trail which follows the top of the ridge and intersects Three Gun Spring Trail 0.6 miles upridge from Post Pass. The second alternative is to continue on up Embudo Canyon proper to the northeast. After passing a waterfall, continue to follow the upper part of the canyon which eventually intersects Three Gun Spring Trail about ¾ mile north of the first junction. Both junctions with Three Gun Spring Trail are marked by Forest Service signs. There is usually water in upper Embudo Canyon below the second Three Gun Spring Trail junction, and it is always present in the lower canyon near the beginning of the trail. Total hiking time up Embudo Trail is two to five hours.

Three Gun Spring Trail

Maintained. Length from trailhead to Oso Pass is 4.0 miles. Elevation gain to Oso Pass is 2,100 feet. This trail is one of several which are frequently used for access to the South Sandia Peak area. The upper half of the trail is often traveled by hikers who start from Embudo Canyon and join Three Gun Spring Trail on the way up. To reach the trailhead travel east on Interstate 40 and take the Carnuel exit continuing east on old Highway 66. At a point about 3.5 miles east of Tramway Road turn north into a small residential area, continuing until the road ends. From this point, the trail goes north up the dry

Old juniper tree below South Peak. Photo by Mike Hill.

arroyo. After one mile the trail steepens and enters a series of switchbacks which lead to the crest of the ridge to the left. Just up the arroyo from the base of the switchbacks is Three Gun Spring for which the trail is named. The spring allegedly got its name from the three pistols carved into an old nearby watering trough.

At the top of the ridge is the first of two junctions with trails leading up from Embudo Canyon. From this point the forest cover is heavier and the hiking becomes even more pleasant. The trail continues to climb to the north and after about one mile it crosses a small stream fed by a usually dependable spring. This is the second Embudo Canyon Trail junction. Continue on the uphill branch of the trail; the downhill branch leads back down Embudo Canyon. One mile farther is the Embudito Trail junction at Oso Pass. From Oso Pass the hiker can either

Rappellers in Embudo Canyon. Photo by David Benyak.

hike 3.0 miles down Embudito Trail or continue up Embudito Trail 1.3 miles to Deer Pass which is about half a mile south of South Sandia Peak. A short distance beyond Deer Pass is the intersection with the Crest Trail.

South Crest Trail

Maintained. The 16-mile Crest Trail is the longest trail in the Sandias. It runs along the ridgeline from Tijeras Canyon at the south to Sandia Crest at the north. When combined with the North Crest Trail, this network covers the entire length of the Sandias from Tijeras Canyon to Placitas, a distance of just over 28 miles. Total elevation gain from the Canyon Estates trailhead to Sandia Crest is 4,000 feet. Along the length of the Crest Trail are numerous intersections with various side trails. These include the Embudito, Cañoncito, Cienega, Tree Spring, Embudo Cave, Faulty, and La Luz trails. An excellent hike can be planned using a section of the Crest Trail as a connector between two of these side trails.

The Canyon Estates trailhead is the standard starting point for the South Crest Trail. To reach the trailhead, exit Interstate 40 at the Tijeras exit. At the stop sign go left, under the overpass, and continue right on the dead-end road past the Canyon Estates residential area until you reach a small parking area.

For the first several miles, the South Crest Trail approaches the crest ridge and elevation gain is fairly sustained, after a short initial section, all the way to South Peak. On the lower part of the trail you bypass a travertine or soda formation and at about the four-mile point the hiker arrives at South Point—a nice lookout at the south end of the west escarpment. Farther on, the trail passes through the vicinity of South Sandia Spring (you will have to hike down to it, and it is sometimes dry) and about a mile and a half up the trail you should come to the Embudito Trail junction, just to the east of Deer Pass. The Crest Trail continues below and to the east of South Sandia Peak and from this point the elevation gain lessens and you can concentrate more on enjoying the hike. North of South Peak the trail will pass a usable emergency shelter, called Bear Shelter. On this section the trail stays just below the crest ridge and there are many opportunities to walk up to the ridge for a scenic view. About three miles north of South Peak you reach the intersection with Cañoncito Trail and a mile farther is the Cienega Trail intersection. In the remaining distance to the upper tram terminal you will pass the intersection of the Tree Spring and 10 K trails; the last mile to the tram terminal is the final leg burner of the hike. Just over a mile past the tram terminal you will come to Sandia Crest, the high elevation point of the trail. If you wish to brave the tourists at the crest (standard question: "Did you hike all the way up the mountain?") you can purchase a soft drink at the gift shop.

If you are continuing the entire length of the Crest Trail proceed north past the communication towers either on the access road or on the trail constructed just below the towers. The remainder of the trail to the north coincides with the North Crest Trail so the description won't be repeated here. If adventure is your game you can try to reconstruct the scrub oaks bushwhack north from the head of Del Agua Canyon. This was once a necessary part of the hike before the North Crest Trail was constructed but it isn't recommended. While the entire length of the Crest Trail can be done in one day by a strong hiker traveling light and hiking fast, plan on one to two days to make it to Sandia Crest and two to three days to do the entire trail. Unless you can talk someone out of some water at Sandia Crest or the upper tram terminal, plan on carrying all the water along that you will need as none is likely to be available.

North Crest Trail

Maintained. Length is 12.2 miles from Tunnel Spring to Sandia Crest. Net altitude gain over this distance is 4,300 feet. This is a new trail completed in 1976. It runs from Tunnel Spring, near Placitas, to Sandia Crest and combines with the South Crest Trail to cover the entire length of the Sandia Mountains.

The north trailhead is at Tunnel Spring, the site of an abandoned fish hatchery near Placitas. To reach Tunnel

Spring, drive east on Highway 44 from Interstate 25 about five miles and turn south on Forest Road No. 231, just before reaching the town of Placitas (a Forest Service sign marks the turnoff). This 1.9-mile road leads directly to Tunnel Spring and the trailhead.

The trail begins east of the parking area. It makes a broad loop to the east and swings back around to gain the head of Del Orno Canyon. A short distance farther on (about four miles from the trailhead) is an overlook on the east rim of Agua Sarca Canyon. On several occasions up to this point, the trail crosses an old jeep road which is located in the same general area. From the Agua Sarca overlook, the trail wanders around on the east slope before emerging into the scrub oak about 1.5 or 2 miles farther up the trail. The trail continues on up through the scrub oak to the crest ridge. Once the ridge is gained, the trail continues south past Del Agua overlook (where the road intersects the trail) and continues south along the rim another 2.5 miles past the radio towers to the crest. From Sandia Crest one can continue south on the South Crest Trail. The only water available along the entire length of the trail is at Tunnel Spring where the trail begins, or at the mouth of Tunnel Canyon a short distance farther on.

For a reasonably significant shortcut, hike directly up Del Orno Canyon rather than taking the broad loop to the east on the lower part of the trail. To find the trail up Del Orno Canyon, take the first branch to the right off the Tunnel Spring Trail a short distance from the trailhead. This branch leads up the lower part of the canyon past a small stream and begins to wind its way up the west side of the canyon. The trail stays generally on the west side of the canyon until it switches to the east side near the top and intersects the regular Tunnel

Spring Trail a short distance farther on at the head of the canyon. The shortcut trail is steep and rough and gets a bit faint near the top. However, it cuts perhaps as much as three miles off the maintained trail and can save considerable time, particularly on the way down.

Faulty Trail

Maintained. This trail runs north-south and connects the lower South Crest Trail with Cañoncito Spring 4.7 miles to the north. It is reputed to be part of an old pack trail which provided access from Tijeras Canyon to the North Sandia Peak area before the present road system was established. The trail was surreptitiously cleared or recleared by unknown persons in 1975, and later the Forest Service incorporated it into its trail system. Also formerly known as the Mystery Trail and the Diamond Trail, Faulty Trail is named for a geological fault line that it follows part of the way.

One usually starts the Faulty Trail at the south end by branching off the South Crest Trail at one of two junctions. The original junction occurs just over two miles up the South Crest Trail where the trail reaches a small mesa at about 7,600 feet and turns back sharply to the south. A more direct access to the Faulty Trail begins lower down on the South Crest Trail and is described as follows. Just before the trail crosses left over a creek bed, at ½ to ¾ mile from the start of the South Crest Trail, you will come to a trail marker. Faulty Trail cuts north up a hillside at this point and is marked with a diamond-shaped blaze on a tree about 30 feet up from the trail intersection. These distinctive diamond blazes continue to mark the trail along its entirety. After an initial elevation gain the trail follows a fairly level contour. It is well marked and easy to follow. There is a spring along the way near an old hollowed-out log that is usually dry; the only dependable source of water along the trail is at Cañoncito Spring at the north end of the trail. From Cañoncito Spring you can either hike up the Cañoncito Trail to the South Crest Trail and make a loop back down the South Crest Trail, or retrace your route on the Faulty Trail. Hiking time from Canyon Estates to Cañoncito Spring is two to four hours.

Cañoncito Trail

Maintained. Length is 3 miles. Elevation gain is 2,200 feet. Hiking time from bottom to top is 1½ to 3 hours. The trailhead is reached by traveling 3.5 miles north from Interstate 40 on Highway 14. Turn left on a dirt road named Cole Springs Road which takes you to Cañoncito and Cole Springs Picnic Grounds. Follow this road keeping right at the first fork and staying left at the second fork. Before Cole Springs Picnic Area there will be a sign on the west side of the road marking the entrance to the Cañoncito Trail.

The trail is well worn all the way to the top. The elevation gain is gentle for the first 0.8 mile until Cañoncito Spring. This spring is usually flowing. After the spring, the hiking becomes more strenuous; however, it is a beautiful hike with a profusion of wildflowers and wild strawberries all along the upper part of the trail. At the top, just beyond the intersection with the Crest Trail, is a very good view of Bear Canyon. One can continue either north or south along the Crest Trail or return along Cañoncito Trail.

In winter, the Forest Service may close the Cole Springs Picnic Area and the Cañoncito trailhead to motor vehicle traffic.

Cienega Spring Trail

Maintained. Length from trailhead to Crest Trail is 2.3 miles. Net elevation gain is 1,700 feet. The trailhead is marked by a Forest Service sign and is located at the upper end of the Cienega Canyon Picnic Area. You reach the picnic area by driving approximately 1.8 miles on Highway 44 past the Highway 14 junction. Turn left at the Cienega Canyon-Sulphur Canyon turnoff, and continue for nearly a mile to the picnic area. The trailhead is at the end of the pavement just past the picnic area. In winter the picnic area may be closed necessitating a short hike to the trailhead. Located just past the trailhead, Cienega Spring provides a dependable source of water, although water may be found farther up the canyon during many parts of the year. The trail is well marked and approximately follows the main canyon all the way up—not the more northerly route as marked on the topo map. The first half mile of the trail has a rather gentle altitude gain but it climbs more steeply during the remainder of the hike. At the top, the trail joins the Crest Trail at a small saddle in the ridge. From this point is a spectacular view of Bear, Pino, and Domingo Baca canyons. Allow one and a half to three hours to hike all the way up and one or two hours to return.

Tree Spring Trail

Maintained. Length of trail is 1.8 miles with an elevation gain of 880 feet. The trailhead is located off Highway 44, 5.7 miles north of the Highway 14 junction. A sign on the west side of the road marks the trailhead. The trail makes its way up the forested east side of the mountain just south of the ski area, and intersects the Crest Trail near the head of Pino Canyon. Hiking time is ½ to 2 hours. Water is sometimes available at Tree Spring several hundred feet south on Highway 44 from the trailhead, but is otherwise unavailable along the trail.

Embudo Cave Trail

Unmaintained. This trail begins on the west side of Highway 44 about half a mile south of the ski area and ends just below the Summit House. For the first half mile the trail is well marked as it leads past Embudo Cave, a cave with archeological possibilities which has been blocked with an iron gate. From the cave, the remaining 2.5 miles of trail are seldom traveled and not easy to find. The trail is cut by ski runs—the upper part coincides with the ski run beneath the chairlift. The trail is quite difficult to pick up from the top end. In general this trail makes a nice dayhike, but one must be prepared to make his way up ski runs on the steep upper half.

10 K Trail

Maintained. This trail is part of an old trail system that traversed the east side of the Sandia Mountains. The south terminus is at the junction of the South Crest and Tree Spring trails. The trail contours north, incorporating the old Osha Spring Trail and ends by intersecting the North Crest Trail in the vicinity of North Sandia Peak. The trail gets its name from the fact that it ends at the 10,000-foot elevation level after a 600-foot elevation gain along the way. The length of the 10 K

Trail is almost 5 miles with an additional 1½ miles required to reach the trailhead at the south end. Total hiking time is 2½ to 5 hours each way.

The trail can be started either by hiking 1½ miles south
from Sandia Crest on the South Crest Trail to the Tree
Spring Trail junction or by hiking a similar distance up
the Tree Spring Trail to the same trail junction. Although
not presently identified by trail markers, the 10 K Trail
heads north on a level contour through the scrub oak
and continues north for 2.3 miles to the crest road.
Along the way the trail crosses several ski runs and care
must be taken to look for blaze marks or tin can lids
nailed to trees which locate where the trail reenters the
forest on the other side of the ski runs. At the crest
road, cross a rough jeep road on the south side of the
pavement and continue on the trail marked by blazes to
the broad clearing which runs north-south. Cross the
clearing and walk across to the north side of the paved
crest road. The trail picks up again in the woods about
50 feet west of the broad roadcut clearing. This is the
beginning of what was formerly called the Osha Spring
Trail. The trail continues north from this point for about
two miles to a cross trail and a sign which points east
and is presently labeled "Osha Spring." This sign is mis-
labeled because of an error on the U.S.G.S. topo map
and should point out Media Spring which lies a short
distance down the cross trail. Returning to the above
trail intersection at the sign, the 10 K Trail continues left
and up for less than a mile, crossing the roadcut clearing (look for a blaze on a tree marking the trail at the
west side of the clearing), and joins the North Crest
Trail. This marks the end of the 10 K Trail. At the North
Crest Trail junction the hiker can return either by hiking
back via the Crest Trail, dropping back down to the
roadcut clearing which leads back to the crest road (two

switchbacks up the road from the previous crossing), or by looping back by way of the Osha Loop Trail.

Osha Loop Trail

Osha Loop Trail is a new trail which branches off the 10 K Trail, loops past Media and Osha springs, and returns to its starting point using segments of the North Crest and 10 K trails. Its total length is just under 3.5 miles and it has an elevation gain of about 800 feet. Hiking time for the loop is 1½ to 3 hours. The trail at present is not well marked in places so allow some time for route finding. You can reach the Osha Loop Trail either by hiking north from Sandia Crest on the North Crest Trail or by hiking north on the 10 K Trail from the crest road. For purposes of this description it will be assumed that the hiker is using the 10 K Trail approach. It is also appropriate at this point to detail some errors on the U.S.G.S. Sandia Crest topo map. Media Canyon should be labeled Las Huertas Canyon, Osha Spring and Osha Canyon should be labeled Media Spring and Media Canyon, with Osha Canyon the next major canyon north of Media Canyon. Now that confusion is undoubtedly complete we shall proceed to the trail description.

The Osha Loop Trail begins as an easterly offshoot from the 10 K Trail about two miles north of the crest road. A sign pointing to Osha Spring (should be Media Spring) currently marks this intersection. Hiking down the trail you should pass above the spring as the trail contours north and climbs out of the north side of the canyon. This part of the trail toward Osha Canyon is very faint with numerous clearings and it is imperative to watch for the rock cairns which mark the way. After about one mile you cross a jeep road. The trail continues left up the old jeep road and skirts the upper end of Osha Canyon. (If one wishes to find Osha Spring, hike down the jeep road then left on a fork several hundred feet down. Follow this fork north then drop down into Osha Canyon.) As you pass above Osha Canyon the old jeep road gradually fades out and you continue on a faint trail with several large switchbacks until you come to a broad roadcut clearing. Some searching may be necesssary to locate the trail on the other side of the clearing. Follow the trail up a short distance more to the intersection with the North Crest Trail, presently marked with a rock cairn. Head back south on the North Crest Trail almost ¼ mile until you pass a pair of stone benches which overlook the south fork of Del Agua Canyon. The trail heads back down into the forest a short distance past the stone benches, again crosses the road, and works its way down to the original starting point. Finish by following the 10 K Trail back south to your original point of departure at the crest road.

Sandia Man Cave Trail

Maintained. This short half-mile trail is reached by driving south 5 or 6 miles from Placitas on Highway 44 or by driving north on Highway 44 past the crest road. From the parking area east of the road, the trail traverses up the east side of Las Huertas Canyon and ends at the Sandia Man Cave.

Sandia Man Cave is a registered National Historic Landmark and one of the most significant early-man sites in this part of the country. Excavated from 1936 through 1940, the cave was found to contain three separate cultural strata. The top level contained artifacts from the Pueblo III Period (A.D. 1050 to 1400). The second layer of debris resulted from Folsom Man's occupation

(6000 to 7000 B.C.). This layer included various Folsom points, flint and bone tools, and remains from various prehistoric animals including the horse, camel, bison, mammoth, ground sloth, and wolf. The lowest and earliest level of occupation is perhaps the most significant. Mammoth tusks found at this stratum have been tentatively dated as being 26,000 years old, making the people who occupied the cave at that time among the earliest known inhabitants of the New World. This early inhabitant was given the name Sandia Man, although no remains of him have ever been found. The debris found in the cave, however, includes some of the same type of animal remains as found at the Folsom level, as well as various artifacts including a unique style of stone projectile point.

Cienega Spring Nature Trail for the Handicapped

This trail is located in the Cienega Spring Picnic Area. Reach the picnic area by driving approximately 1.8 miles on Highway 44 past the Highway 14 junction. Turn left at the Cienega Canyon-Sulphur Canyon turnoff and continue to the picnic area.

The nature trail for the handicapped is a short loop trail near the Cienega Springs Picnic Area and just northeast of the obvious meadow. The trail is paved with asphalt to assist wheelchair traffic. As with the Crest Nature Trail, markers along the trail describe various types of forest vegetation. These markers provide information in print and in braille.

Crest Nature Trail and Rim Nature Trail

Two short self-guided nature trails have been developed along the crest. The Rim Nature Trail runs for a short distance along the crest rim, directly south from Sandia Crest, and the Crest Nature Trail runs north from the Summit House. Both trails have a gentle slope and are easy to follow. Markers identifying particular types of forest vegetation have been placed along the trails. These trails are an excellent way for the hiker to familiarize himself with the forest vegetation found in the Sandias.

CROSS-COUNTRY SKIING AND SNOWSHOEING

The winter sports of cross-country skiing and snow-shoeing are becoming increasingly popular forms of recreation in the Sandias. Cross-country skiing in particular has enjoyed a tremendous burst of popularity in recent years. For those who wish to try these activities this section gives some basic information on equipment, technique, and places to go.

Snowshoeing

For self-propelled travel through deep snow snow-shoeing is clearly the easiest technique in which to reach a reasonable degree of proficiency. On open terrain skiing is quicker and has more of an element of thrill (some would substitute the word *terror*) but it does require more basic technique, particularly in turning and stopping. Snowshoeing is a more plodding form of travel but it requires only a little practice and a degree of physical conditioning. Snowshoeing is also generally more adaptable to different types of forest terrain, for a person of moderate experience. Virtually any hiking trail in the Sandias with sufficient snow cover can be snowshoed (more on this later). Sufficient snow cover usually means 8 to 12 inches or more; of course the rockier the subsurface, the more snow required. Inadequate snow cover will result in damage to snowshoes and is easier to negotiate on foot anyway. Snowshoes allow you to leave the trail and create your own path through the woods. This can be very satisfying but avoid travel through thick, brushy forest cover. The term *bushwhacking*—commonly used to describe this form of torture—does not adequately describe the travails involved in negotiating brush, deadfall, and steep gullies with snowshoes strapped to your feet. Better to flagellate yourself with a wet rope.

The most versatile snowshoe for the Sandias is about 10 inches wide and 36 to 46 inches long. A shorter and wider snowshoe is good for negotiating thick brush but more tiring for sustained travel. A long snowshoe is most appropriate for deep snow in moderate, open terrain. The better snowshoes are of wood or aluminum frame with either neoprene or rawhide lacing. The best bindings, used to attach the snowshoes to your feet, are made of neoprene-nylon laminate. One piece of equipment that many snowshoers find handy is a cross-country ski pole with a large powder basket used either singly or by the pair. The ski pole gives you, in effect, a third leg and is handy in getting up steep spots. Appropriate footwear is any kind of warm, water-resistant boots that are compatible with the snowshoe bindings. Read the comments on clothing in the hiking section. Additional clothing should include snow gaiters, preferably knee high, and of course, a pair of warm mitts.

As previously mentioned, any hiking trail with sufficient snow cover can be snowshoed. However, since
many of the trails often don't have enough snow, I will
point out a few of the better ones. The North Crest Trail
is always always good from Sandia Crest past North Del
Agua Lookout. The South Crest Trail between Sandia
Crest and the upper tram terminal is good but has heavy
cross-country ski traffic; likewise for the road segment
between the lower parking lot at Sandia Crest and Kiwanis Meadow. The South Crest Trail south of the tram
terminal to South Peak is good but has some steep spots.
Tree Spring and Cienega Spring Trails always have good
snow cover and are steep enough to discourage skiers.
You will have to carry your snowshoes part of the way
to reach the Cienega Spring trailhead as the picnic area
is blocked off in winter. The roadcut opposite the tram
terminal service road is also good all the way to North
Del Agua overlook, as is that portion of the 10 K Trail
north of the crest road. Most of the other trails are not
appropriate for a variety of reasons including inadequate snow on part or all of the trail, inaccessible trailheads, and heavy ski traffic. Avoid in particular that
portion of the La Luz Trail which leads to the upper
tram terminal as there are often icy patches above exposed cliffs. Avoid also the service road between the upper tram terminal and the crest road. This has by far the
most cross-country ski traffic on the mountain and the
skiers will appreciate your not marring the ski tracks
with your snowshoes.

Remember that it takes longer to snowshoe a trail than
to hike it in summer. There are fewer daylight hours and
trails are often trickier to follow in several feet of snow.
Leave your itinerary with someone, and make sure you
are equipped to survive a night in the woods if necessary. If you are interested in trying snowshoeing in the

Cross country skier heading south on the South Crest Trail. Photo by Carl Smith.

Sandias, the Forest Service offers guided snowshoe hikes. The New Mexico Mountain Club also schedules snowshoe hikes. If you don't own snowshoes, you can rent them at several backpacking shops in Albuquerque or from the Sandia Peak Tram Company.

Cross-Country Skiing

While there are parts of the state that offer a more dependable supply of snow and perhaps better terrain, the Sandias offer skiing conditions that vary from fair to excellent and the close proximity to Albuquerque provides unbeatable convenience. Cross-country skiing in the Sandias is concentrated on the upper reaches of the mountain where the snow cover is good and trails are relatively gentle. While not technically a part of the Rocky Mountain chain, the Sandias receive snow that is typical of the Rockies. Fresh snow is light and powdery and remains so under forest cover for most of the winter. Snow in open spaces tends to become hard packed and icy as warmer weather sets in. This poses a classic waxing problem as the season wears on. Waxable skis probably sell best in the area but no-wax skis are popular and can be very useful, particularly in late winter or early spring. The most prevalent form of cross-country skiing is, of course, general recreational. A small group of cross-country ski racers has been active for years, and at the other extreme there has been significant interest in telemark skiing which is primarily done on the alpine ski runs. There are various races and contests scheduled throughout the winter for the various forms of cross-country skiing. A discussion of cross-country ski equipment and technique is beyond the scope of this book. My advice is to consult a knowledgeable salesperson in one of the local shops that specialize in the sport.

Most cross-country skiing is done, as you might expect, on trails. A few of the established hiking trails are suitable, but a number of trails are specifically maintained for cross-country skiing. In accordance with several national ski associations, the Forest Service has adopted a standard set of signs to identify the trails and degree of difficulty. Although most of the Sandia ski trails are not presently marked with the standard symbols, some will eventually be identified with the cross-country skier symbol and marked with blue diamonds to identify the route. Listed below are a number of the trails most suitable for cross-country skiing. Included for each trail is a brief description along with length and level of difficulty in categories of easy, intermediate, or advanced. Refer to the ski trail map for trail locations.

Crest Trail in winter, looking south towards Kiwanis Hut. Photo by Carl Smith.

North Crest Trail

Length is 2.1 miles to South Del Agua overlook or 3.3 miles to North Del Agua overlook. The trail begins opposite the parking area at Sandia Crest a short distance down from the communication towers access road. The first part of the trail is easy but it gets more difficult farther north. Snow cover is good but the trail is narrow and has difficult spots. Return the same way or via the roadcut clearing.

South Crest Trail

Length from Sandia Crest to the upper tram terminal is about 1.5 miles and is intermediate in difficulty. South of the tram terminal the trail is steeper and not often

Skiing in lower Kiwanis Meadow. Photo by Carl Smith.

skied. This part requires advanced skiing ability. Snow cover is good but the trail between Sandia Crest and the tram terminal may have less than ideal snow because of the heavy ski and foot traffic, not to mention numerous sitzmarks. Enter the trail south of the giftshop at Sandia Crest, or more commonly, at the south end of Kiwanis Meadow via the Kiwanis Meadow Road. You can also start at the south end just north of the tram terminal.

Kiwanis Meadow Road

Length is 0.5 mile. This trail is easy and popular for learning to ski. The trail starts at the south end of the lower parking lot at Sandia Crest. It continues down, skirting the northwest side of Kiwanis Meadow and ending in the vicinity of Kiwanis Hut.

Buried Cable Trail

Length is about half a mile to Kiwanis Meadow. Difficulty rating is intermediate. This is a narrow and exciting trail with good snow cover. The trail starts at the northeast corner of the lower parking lot at Sandia Crest and exits at the far north end of Kiwanis Meadow. From this point either turn left and ski down to the service road after reaching the crest road, or continue across Kiwanis Meadow and ski to the tram terminal via either the service road or the South Crest Trail.

Service Road

Length is about one mile. This is probably the easiest ski trail on the mountain and also the most heavily skied. The road catches a lot of sun so snow conditions vary according to the freshness of the snow. The service road provides access from the crest road to the upper tram terminal; one usually starts at the south end just northeast of the tram terminal.

Challenge Route

Length is 0.9 mile to the crest road at the first major clearing or 4.3 miles if taken to the base of the downhill ski area. Snow cover is good on the upper part of the trail but may be marginal on the lower section. The trail starts just north of the gate at the north end of the service road. Ski east from the service road and down, ending with an exciting run onto a large clearing which you can follow north to the crest road and then carry your skis back up. The portion of the trail described thus far is of intermediate difficulty. The lower portion of the trail generally follows the crest road to the base of

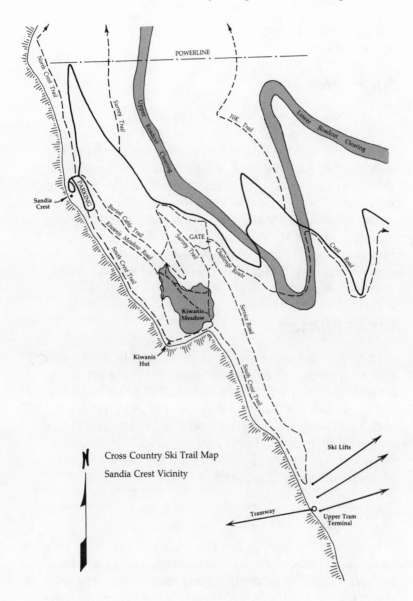

Cross Country Ski Trail Map
Sandia Crest Vicinity

the downhill ski area. This part of the trail requires an advanced skier.

Survey Trail

Length is 0.35 mile from the service road to the crest road or 2.2 miles if taken to South Del Agua overlook. Difficulty is easy to intermediate. This trail starts at the service road just south of the gate on the west side of the road. Continue up on easy terrain, bearing to the right until you come to the crest road. On the north side of the road opposite the vegetation sign, the trail picks up again and continues north for 1.6 miles to the junction of the 10 K and North Crest trails at South Del Agua overlook. The trail is narrow and snow cover is good.

Upper Roadcut

Length is 3.4 miles from the crest road to North Del Agua overlook. It is generally easy but there are some steep icy sections. This broad roadcut clearing begins at the crest road opposite the north end of the service road and roller coasters its way north to North Del Agua overlook. It is windblown and exposed to the sun so snow conditions are variable. When the snow is good it is fun to ski and a good workout.

10 K Trail

Length is 2.0 miles from the crest road to the Osha Loop Trail. Difficulty level is advanced. This is a narrow trail with difficult places but good snow cover. The trail starts on the north side of the crest road three switch-backs down from the top, a short distance uphill from the broad roadcut clearing. The trail heads north for two miles to a fork where the 10 K Trail continues left and the Osha Loop Trail takes off to the right. At this point you will probably want to return, but if you like climbing on steep terrain, the trail to the left will take you up across the upper roadcut clearing to the North Crest Trail. The Osha Loop Trail is not recommended.

Capulin Trail

Length is 1.1 miles. This is an easy trail which may or may not have good snow conditions because of its lower elevation. The trail begins 0.2 miles north of the Sandia Crest turnoff on Highway 44 and heads west past the Capulin Picnic Area and makes a loop which ends at the crest road.

Remember that the difficulty ratings assigned to the above trails are general and can vary significantly with the condition of the snow. If you haven't learned any other ski technique, at least know to sit down and stop when the situation demands. Reread the comments in the hiking section concerning clothing and routefinding, and keep in mind that an injury on a remote trail can turn a skiing trip into a survival situation. Ski solo at your own risk. If you want a group skiing experience but don't have the group, the New Mexico Ski Touring Club offers an excellent opportunity for skiers of all levels. Finally, if you would like to obtain more information on skiing opportunities in the local area, the best source available is a copy of *Ski Touring in Northern New Mexico* by Sam Beard.

CLIMBING IN THE SANDIAS

WARNING
Rock climbing is a dangerous sport if attempted without the proper equipment, climbing techniques, and experience in using them. None of the climbs described in this section should be attempted without adequate training and equipment.

Most climbers are aware of the continuing controversy concerning guidebooks so we won't discuss all the pros and cons. This section is written to assist local climbers by providing standardized information on existing climbing routes and we feel that the advantages of providing this information outweigh the disadvantages. More specifically, the guidebook will help a climber evaluate the difficulty of the various routes relative to his climbing ability. This will help him use his climbing time more efficiently, may keep him out of trouble, and should familiarize him with a larger number of routes.

Just as important, the guidebook identifies contemporary attitudes concerning climbing ethics. We hope to increase the climber's awareness of his impact upon the rock environment and consideration of his fellow climber.

Location of Climbs

Areas for rock climbing in the Sandia Mountains are somewhat scattered, but most are in the rugged western escarpment between the Shield to the north and Domingo Baca Canyon to the south. Climbs outside this area are relatively few and usually particularly difficult in their approaches. The climbs are concentrated on prominent geographical formations such as the Shield, the Needle, and the Prow or clustered in areas such as upper La Cueva Canyon. Approaches to these various areas can be rather strenuous and usually take anywhere from 30 minutes to 2 hours. The approaches are discussed in more detail in the section on route descriptions.

Climbing Seasons

Roped climbing in the Sandias is generally done from April to early November, although climbing is theoretically possible any month of the year, especially at the lower elevations. When climbing in spring one must contend with cold temperatures, fewer daylight hours, and winds which can reach high velocities on exposed ridges. Temperatures during the summer and early fall are usually quite pleasant although more drinking water is needed during this period. Rainfall is heaviest from mid-July to mid-September. Winter brings snow, cold winds, and temperatures which average below freezing, although occasional warm spells can produce enjoyable climbing in lower elevations such as Embudo Canyon or lower La Cueva Canyon.

The Rock

Virtually all climbing in the Sandias is done on granite. Since the quality of this granite varies significantly from climb to climb, it is a major factor and has been included in most route descriptions. Since many of the routes will have some loose rock, climbing helmets are recommmended—particularly for the second on the rope.

Clean Climbing

Clean climbing is a term which has been much talked about in recent years and is widely accepted in the local climbing community. The emphasis on clean climbing received its big push in the major climbing areas of the country where some of the more popular climbs have been eroded by the accumulated damage from insertion and removal of countless pitons. Although the Sandias might never have the concentration of climbers to produce the kind of damage which has occurred on Bishops' Roof or Serenity Crack, clean climbing is still a valid concept. Most free climbs in the area rely primarily on nuts for protection. Some climbs still have old pitons and bolts placed in various locations. Although many of these were not planned as fixed protection, pitons and bolts necessary to protect difficult moves should be left in place. Unnecessary and/or unsafe piton placements should be removed. Bolts may just as well be left in place in any case since a chopped bolt is just as ugly as one left intact. In general, it is just not justified to carry a bolt kit along, particularly when climbing an existing route. One reason that bolts and drills are not sold in the local climbing shops is that many of the potential purchasers have no business using them.

A word of caution: occasionally there is a lead which cannot be protected well using only nuts, exotic load equalizing systems using several tiny stoppers notwithstanding. Clean climbing is an admirable form but it must be taken in its proper perspective. The choice between taking a short leader fall on a piton and taking a long fall on your last nut placement is obvious. A good rule to follow is to use nuts to protect whenever possible, but use pitons before subjecting you and your climbing partner to unnecessary risk due to inadequate protection. Hopefully, all routes which require bolts or pitons will eventually have them fixed in the appropriate locations. In the route descriptions, assume that the route can be climbed using only nuts unless otherwise indicated, although some climbers prefer to carry along a few pitons just in case. If you decide to carry a few pitons to complement a nut rack, concentrate on thin pitons such as knife blades and Lost Arrows since a thin crack is often the hardest to protect or aid using nuts.

First Ascents

After some thought and discussion we decided to include credits for first ascents in appendix form (Appendix E). The alternatives were to include the credits in the appropriate route description or to omit them altogether. Although it is of historical interest to know when and by whom various routes were first done there are several reasonable arguments for not including this information. First, knowing who did the first ascent really does not affect the enjoyment of the climb and provides no useful information about the climb. Secondly, many popular climbs in the Sandias were first done by unknown individuals. Finally, the possibility of being immortalized in a guidebook undoubtedly encourages some climbers to put up superfluous routes without regard to natural line or quality of climb. However, in deference to the historical aspect we have compromised and chosen the appendix solution.

A climbing route justifies inclusion in a guidebook only if there is a reasonable probability that other climbers will want to repeat the route. The primary criteria for this determination are such considerations as the natural line of the climb, the difficulty of the climb, the quality of the rock, and the reasonableness of the approach. Several of the routes that appeared in the previous edition but which have attracted no subsequent attention have been eliminated or abbreviated in this edition. First ascent credits, however, have been left intact in the appendix.

Naming of Routes

Traditionally, climbing routes in the Sandias have been named according to their physical location on a given formation—for example, the Northwest Ridge of the Prow, the Northwest Ridge of the Thumb, West Face of the Chimney, and so on. Some routes have not been named but are designated merely by a number. To reduce the dullness of it all, people responsible for first ascents are encouraged to name their routes with a bit of originality. This will also become something of a necessity as more routes are put up.

Rescue

Several rescue groups with varying areas of expertise

are active in the Albuquerque area. The best procedure for rescue during working hours is to call the Forest Service Ranger Station for the Sandia District. The station is located on Highway 14 about a mile south of Interstate 40, phone 281-3304. The Forest Service can then contact the appropriate group or groups. If an emergency occurs during nonworking hours, contact the State Police or County Sheriff's Department. Mountain rescue can best be facilitated if the climber has left word of the exact location of his proposed climb and his estimated time of return.

Rating Systems

Rating sytems have evolved to describe a climb in terms of length, difficulty, and sustention of difficulty. As with any rating system inconsistency results from variations in individual perception and psychological makeup. There is also the problem of rating face climbs along with crack climbs, and so on. However, the need for some kind of a rating system clearly exists and the local climbing community has gradually adopted the system used by major climbing areas of the country which rate climbs by grade and class. These are more fully explained as follows:

Grade—This rating on a scale of I to VI classifies a climb as to the average time it takes to complete. This relates directly to both the length of the climb and how sustained the climb is in its severity. Grades I through IV apply to an average climber; grades V and VI apply to expert climbers since they will normally be the only ones capable of doing climbs of this length and severity. The specific grades are:

Grade I: Up to several hours, usually no more than two leads.

Grade II: Up to half a day, average of three to five leads.

Grade III: Most of a day, can be four to six leads or more.

Grade IV: One full day to one and a half days.

Grade V: More than one day. This grade applies only to an expert climber rather than an average climber.

Grade VI: More than two days.

Class—This rating classifies a climb or hike according to its maximum difficulty. The system used here is usually called the decimal or Yosemite system. Despite the sources of inconsistency mentioned earlier, experienced climbers within a given area usually agree on rating various climbs or differ by one decimal point at the most. Since many climbs described in this book have been done by only a few people, many of the ratings have not been established by consensus, so there probably is some variation in the difficulty ratings.

The class ratings are structured as follows:

Class 1: Easy hiking

Class 2: Difficult hiking with longer distances and more elevation gain involved.

Class 3: Rugged off-trail scrambling or very easy climbing with occasional use of handholds and footholds. Exposure may be significant and a rope is sometimes used.

Class 4: Rugged, exposed scrambling or easy climbing. A rope is usually used along with anchored belays.

Class 5: Technical climbing with significant exposure. A rope is considered essential as are nuts, slings, or pitons to protect the leader. Class 5 is broken down by decimal from 5.0 to 5.12. 5.0 is the easiest technical climbing, very difficult to separate from Class 4, and 5.12 is the most difficult technical climbing currently considered possible. Spiderman climbs 5.13.

Class A: This rating denotes *aid climbing* (i.e, using

artificial holds, pitons, nuts, etc., as a means of progression) and is broken down from A1 to A5. Also used is the rating A0. A0 indicates the use of minimal aid such as standing on a piton, use of a tension traverse, or taking a boost from your climbing partner. A1 aid involves nuts or pitons that are very solid and easy to place. A2 aid is relatively easy to place and solid enough to hold a short fall. A3 involves awkward or strenuous placements which may require considerable ingenuity but which should support body weight and maybe even a short fall. A4 is similar to A3 but with less secure placements that will, at best, hold body weight. A5 is the most difficult aid currently considered possible. A5 usually consists of several A4 placements in succession and is a guaranteed zipper in the event of a fall. When applicable, the aid rating is always used in conjunction with the fifth-class rating so that the difficulty of both the aid and freeclimbing sections of the route can be noted; for example—Class 5.8, A2.

The grade and class of a climb are noted respectively, immediately after the name of the route in the route description. As an example, the Northwest Ridge of the Thumb designation would be: NORTHWEST RIDGE, III, 5.5.

Climbing Route Information

Climbing has always required a certain amount of climbing ability and routefinding skill—qualities that cannot be replaced by a guidebook. This is fortunate because guidebooks, by nature if not intent, are of limited usefulness to the climber. As with most guidebooks, this book inevitably contains its share of errors and vacuous references in the route descriptions. In some cases the route description may do little more than point out the general area through which the route goes, and inconsistencies inevitably exist in the ratings given to various routes. These problems occur because of the number of different individuals supplying route information and because most of the route descriptions were reconstructed from memory. So while the route descriptions are an aid, a good deal of personal judgment will be required in doing a route, just as it was for the individuals who first did that route.

For all the climbing routes a certain basic set of information is supplied. This includes the name of the climb, the grade, the class, the extent of difficulty (when available), the number of pitches, and the quality of rock. The climb is rated according to the hardest move on the climb; however, some indication is usually given as to how sustained the more difficult sections are or where the crux moves are located. For example, a three-pitch climb which would be rated 5.2 except for one 5.7 move on the first lead will be rated 5.7, but the difficult lead will usually be identified. For lack of a better reference frame, the climb ratings here correspond fairly closely to those in Yosemite Valley. Since rating climbs is a notoriously subjective undertaking, allow a tolerance of plus or minus one point, especially on a climb like Bird Ridge where there are several possible variations in the route. The number of pitches specified for a climb usually assumes the use of a rope no longer than 150 feet, although most climbs are now being done with 165-foot ropes. Probably the least precise information presented in the route descriptions is quality of rock. The rock is rated either poor, fair, or good to give the reader a crude approximation as to what to expect in the way of loose or broken rock on a particular climb. Approach and descent routes are usually specified for the formation on which the climb is located.

ROUTE DESCRIPTIONS

Del Agua Canyon

This canyon contains a number of formations on which climbs have been done including Beastie, Lady, the Three Pigs, Lobo, and Del Agua Spire. In general, Del Agua Canyon is one of the less-popular climbing areas because of the long approach and the relative lack of good climbs. However, for the determined Del Agua climber, the routes can be approached from several directions. The most common approach is to hike north on the Piedra Lisa Trail from the Juan Tabo area and then bushwhack to the northeast after cresting the Rincon. One can also hike directly up Del Agua Canyon. The final possibility is to hike north from Sandia Crest along the old Crest Trail. The upper part of the South Fork of Del Agua Canyon is just below the north slope of North Sandia Peak. The upper part of the north fork lies ¼ mile to the north.

The Three Pigs in Del Agua Canyon. Photo by David Benyak.

Beastie

The Beastie is the large dome-like pinnacle northeast of the Three Pigs at the extreme upper end of the Del Agua Canyon drainage just below the limestone rim.

Route 1, Zig-Zag, II, 5.6. Midway down the west face from the base of the northwest ridge. Traverse to mid-face and then up a gully to a ledge. Traverse right on this ledge to the southwest ridge. Climb the ridge to a second ledge and traverse back to the northwest ridge. Finish by way of the northwest ridge.

Lady

The Lady is the solitary pinnacle located northwest of

the Beastie. It is shielded on its north side by a large rib which juts from the north slope of the canyon.

Route 1, Northeast Face, I, 5.2. Two pitches.

The Three Pigs

The Three Pigs are the three pinnacles located at the west end of the upper ridge dividing the north and south forks of Del Agua Canyon. They are located about ¾ mile northwest of Del Agua Spire. The easternmost pinnacle of the group, and the largest, is called Big Pig. It and the Middle Pig are the most interesting of the group from a climbing standpoint. The smaller pinnacle to the west is called Little Pig.

Big Pig

Route 1, East Side, I, 5.2. Two pitches. Descend the Big Pig by making two rappels down the east side. The first rappel uses a tree for an anchor.

Route 2, North Side, I, 5.1. Two pitches.

Route 3, West Side, I, 5.4. Two pitches.

Middle Pig

Route 1, East Face, I, 4. One pitch.

Route 2, South Face, I, 5.2. Three pitches.

Little Pig

The Little Pig has been climbed by more than one route. Its south and west sides offer several easy possibilities that are of questionable interest considering the long approach hike.

Lobo

The Lobo is the prominent buttress situated in a northwest-southeast direction and lying northeast of the Three Pigs and south of and across a canyon from Beastie. Its north slope is well forested in contrast to its south side.

Route 1, Northwest Face, I, 5.3.

Del Agua Spire

Del Agua Spire is a prominent pinnacle which is separated by a deep notch from the headwall of the south fork of Del Agua Canyon. It is located almost directly east from the base of the Knife Edge (Shield). Del Agua Spire was once known as the Tooth but this name has fallen into disuse.

Route 1, Southeast Ridge, II, A1.

Route 2, North Face, I, 5.4, A2. One or two pitches. Start at the high point of the notch which separates the spire from the headwall. Climb up about 40 feet and traverse right to a large shelf. From the shelf continue up and left of a wide crack. This crack splits the spire and permits one to look through the rock formation. Quality of rock is good. The crux consists of aid climbing overhanging rock on the first pitch.

Rincon

The Rincon (Spanish for "corner") is the string of small peaks and outcroppings which forms a ridge that travels west from the base of the Shield. Several short climbs are possible on the granite outcroppings but not much interest has been generated because of their relative inaccessability.

Shield

The Shield is the greatest wall in the Sandias. From Albuquerque it is the sheer face that forms the rounded shoulder at what appears to be the north end of the range. Actually, the Shield is a massive rib with both a north and a southwest face. No one knows when climbing first began in the Sandias, but the Shield was one of several prominent formations which were regularly climbed before records were kept. A number of ancient-looking pitons are evidence of the early climbing activity. The Shield was also the site of the first major climbing accident in the Sandias which occurred in 1938 when two apparently novice climbers died while attempting to climb the Knife Edge. Although the Shield has more routes than any other local formation, its formidable size guarantees that more are still to be put up. The broad face of the Shield visible from Albuquerque will be referred to in this book as the southwest face. This face receives most of the climbing attention. The smaller and more inaccessible north face is the wall which forms the north side of the Knife Edge. Climbs described on the Shield are on the southwest face unless otherwise specified.

The approach to the southwest face is generally by hiking north on the Fletcher Trail or up Juan Tabo Arroyo and then making your way up the broad ridge which leads to the center of the face. For climbs on the east end of the face, traverse east on the broad ridge below the Shield to the base of UNM Spire and then up the ramp. The ramp is the huge ledge which starts east of UNM Spire and slopes up the east end of the face. Most of the climbs on this part of the face start from the ramp. Climbs on the east end of the ramp may also be reached by dropping down from the north side of the canyon between the Needle and North Peak. To reach the Knife Edge, the north face, and climbs on the far west end of the south face, one may also hike north from Juan Tabo on the Piedra Lisa Trail and then hike east along the Rincon Spur Trail.

Descent from the Shield can either be accomplished by hiking south along the crest ridge to Sandia Crest and descending by trail or automobile from there, or by performing a sequence of rappels and downclimbings. The following is suggested as one such sequence: from the top of the Knife Edge, traverse east about one-half mile across the top of the main wall. From the bottom of a broad gully at the east end of the Shield rappel 60 feet to a large shelf. Follow the shelf west (do not descend the obvious slopes into the Juan Tabo drainage). At one point a rope is advisable because of considerable exposure and somewhat delicate holds. Shortly after this, one arrives at the broad ramp and follows it down to the streambed, passing several shelter caves under the main wall of the Shield. Either cross the streambed and traverse up to the ridge below the Prow, follow the arroyo south, or return via the Fletcher Trail. Another descent can be accomplished by performing a series of rappels on roughly the same line as followed by Route 5. Do not attempt the latter descent without two 150-foot ropes and at least three hours of remaining daylight.

Route 1, Knife Edge, III, 4. Eleven pitches. Quality of rock is fair to good. The climb is best reached by traveling north on the Piedra Lisa Trail and then east on the Rincon Spur. Most people climb unroped as far as the prominent "W," about two-thirds of the way up. In negotiating the crux of the "W," either traverse to the left around the difficult part or, if you are tall, let yourself down over the ledge by the fingertips. Finish the route several leads farther up and descend by following the

Southwest face of the Shield. Photo by Mike Hill.

Knife Edge back down or by using one of the descent routes previously described.

Route 2, II, 5.6. Five or six pitches. Start at the bottom of the black watermarks below the "W" in the ridge. One long or two short pitches lead to a large platform on top of a shallow buttress. The hardest part of the climb is gaining this platform. Angle left from the platform over a series of easy ledges aiming for the Knife Edge. A short right traverse near the top of the pitch brings you just below the "W." The "W" is not visible from the beginning of the traverse. Upon reaching the "W," follow the Knife Edge to the summit.

Route 3, III, 5.6. Seven pitches. Follow Route 2 as far as the large platform at the end of the second pitch. At this point there will be a series of ledges farther up and to the right. Follow these step-like ledges up until they end. Then cut back to the left and finish just below the summit on the Knife Edge.

Route 4, III, 5.4. Six pitches. This route has the same beginning as the standard S route, however, it branches off to the left a short distance up and follows a ramp up to the left. The route eventually climbs up and comes to the west end of a large group of trees. From here, the original route angled right and gained the summit just to the right of the standard descent route. As an alternative, angle to the left and finish via the upper part of Route 3.

Route 5, Standard S Route, II or III, 5.5. Four or five pitches. Quality of rock is good but with some loose rock in couloirs. Reach the start of the climb either by traversing across from the base of the Knife Edge or by scrambling up via the Fletcher Trail. The climb begins at the highest point of the huge ledge which cuts across the midface of the Shield. After a short section of easy fifth class, scramble to the right on a steep ramp to the

East end of the Shield. Photo by David Benyak.

large group of trees at the top of the ramp. The second lead angles back to the left and up to a second large clump of trees. Continue the climb by climbing straight up and to the right from the second group of trees and following the deep couloir to its end. The last lead then takes a crack system up to the top. The face is surprisingly broken with considerable scrambling between pitches. The last lead is the crux with the first two or three pitches being either fourth or easy fifth class.

Route 6, III, 5.6. Five pitches. Climbing is sustained on the last two pitches, particularly the fourth pitch. Quality of rock is good. This climb begins the same as Route 5; however, instead of turning back to the left at the first large clump of trees, keep scrambling up to the right as far as possible. Then climb straight up to an obvious cave. Traverse left about 100 feet from the cave on a ledge until you come to a steep dihedral. The fourth and crux lead goes up this dihedral which joins Route 5 below the final pitch. Finish the climb as in Route 5.

Route 7, Procrastination, III, 5.8. Eleven pitches. Quality of rock is good to fair. This climb was first done in 1970 to the right of an obvious shallow rib or buttress on the Shield. The climb starts just to the left of the Rainbow overhangs and is reached by hiking up the ramp to the right of a large sloping open book on the right of an overhanging boulder (see also the description for Route 12). Traverse into a large open book and follow this up traversing west under an overhang and up to a steep face. Setting a belay on a smaller ledge up on the face rather than on the larger ledge (which is the end of the second pitch on Chicken Chop Suey) at the base of the face will enable one to reach the next big ledge on the third pitch. The third lead is the crux. From the smaller ledges up and right it goes up a crack at the left corner of the face and traverses right to avoid over-

Dennis Grady on the final pitch of routes 5 and 6 on the Shield. Photo by Carl Smith.

hangs. The rest of the climb is no harder than 5.7 as it continues on various crack systems conveniently located between belay ledges. The upper part of the climb offers several variations. An escape route is located at the ledge at the top of the seventh pitch. From this ledge one can traverse to the west through a small notch to a rappel tree. Three rappels (two ropes required) and some downclimbing lead back down to the ramp. Total time required to do Procrastination is about 11 hours. Approach time to reach the climb is about 2½ hours. Retreat time to the top of the crest is 1½ hours.

Route 8, Smorgasbord, III, 5.6 to 5.8. Six or seven pitches. This unusual climb presents a variety of cracks to ascend and one may choose an ascent with climbing from about 5.6 to 5.9, or harder, although the climbs done are generally in the 5.6-to-5.8 category. Reach the base of the climb by descending down the north side of the canyon between the Needle and North Peak. The climb starts at the base of a large dihedral near the upper end of the ramp. Several open-book cracks may be ascended with the easiest (5.6) on the right and the hardest (5.8) on the left. After three leads you will come to a large grassy ledge. Once you reach this ledge, there are two possibilities for the remainder of the climb. The hard variation is 5.8 and starts directly up a blocky, sloping section past a hard-to-see fixed piton and up a perfect 20-foot open book, with fourth class above the open book. The next lead is 5.7 or 5.8 and continues up a squeeze chimney and around an overhang to the right. Protection is excellent. The final lead is easy fifth class. The easy variation from the midway ledge bears to the right and then makes its way directly up to the top. Protection is a bit more tenuous on this variation.

Route 9, North Face, I, 5.6. Two pitches. Approach by climbing down from the crest ridge. As you drop down from the crest, stay south of the rib located between the Shield and Del Agua Spire. Don't start the climb too high up but wait until you are below the "W" in the Knife Edge. Roped climbing starts on a huge ledge near the top of the trees below the "W." The first lead comes up a crack and then angles off to the left. The next lead goes back to the right and gains the "W." A somewhat easier route starts farther to the right on the large ledge and works its way up to the "W." This alternate route goes perhaps 5.4 or 5.5.

Route 10, Rainbow Route, VI, 5.9, A4. Thirteen pitches. This route leads up through the middle of the two prominent Rainbow overhangs on the Shield. It is possibly the most demanding climb yet accomplished in the Sandias with sustained, difficult free climbing, difficult aid, and several long, poorly protected leadouts. It involves mostly freeclimbing with less than 100 feet of aid. The climb was done with nuts and about a dozen small pitons. Fourteen bolts (placed for belay and protection) may not all have hangers. Two to three days would normally be required to complete the ascent.

Approach the base of the climb by scrambling up the ramp until directly below the Rainbow overhangs. Begin beneath the lower overhang by going over a small bulge beneath a tree. From the tree traverse right beneath a long overhang which diagonals up until it turns into a dihedral. Climb alongside the dihedral before traversing left to a sloping ledge and then up to a belay above some loose-looking blocks. Then go left on a ledge and up a face which is protected by three bolts. Traverse left at the third bolt, then up to a hanging belay at the left end of the little Rainbow overhang. A freeclimb along the overhang leads to its center where a few moves of aid gain a belay spot. Next, climb up to a blocky ledge and belay at the right end of the ledge.

Continue up until beneath the large Rainbow overhang, then go left until you reach a thin, overhanging aid crack. Negotiate the overhang using this crack. Above, a bolt protects a traverse (mostly aid) to the left and then up to a hanging belay beneath a square roof. From the belay, go down and left then up and left to a crack system which leads to a large ledge. From the left end of the ledge wander up and to the right, then back to the left. A protection bolt leads to a small belay ledge. The next two leads go past several trees to the highest ledge with trees. A long traverse to the right ends at the base of a dihedral which is followed to the top.

Route 11, Carrot, IV 5.8, A3. Six pitches; very sustained. The hardest aid is on the second pitch, the hardest freeclimb is on the sixth pitch. This climb is located on the northwest end of the Shield. Reach the climb either by scrambling up via the Fletcher Trail or Juan Tabo Arroyo, or by traversing across from the Rincon Spur Trail. Start the climb in a left-facing dihedral 50 feet to the right of a shelter cave and beneath the overhangs formed by the carrot-shaped formation above. Climb up the dihedral to the ledge on top of the buttress where a bolt is placed for a belay.

The next lead involves 20 feet of freeclimbing, then aid straight up to reach a bolt. Continue up past a dangerously loose block on the left, then move delicately up over and left for 15 feet. Continue up over the smooth slab which is protected by bolts to a small overhang with a fixed piton. Go through this roof via the obvious crack in the left side to a belay ledge with two bolts.

The third lead goes up 15 feet to the top of a ramp and then mixed free and aid climbing leads to a belay stance in a V-shaped alcove directly beneath the "Carrot." The fourth lead goes right, then up to a ramp. Follow the ramp as it steepens, ending in a dead tree, and set a belay beneath the huge right-facing dihedral above. A fixed piton is located here.

The next lead goes up 15 feet, traverses up and right 30 feet, then back up left to within six feet of the corner. Make an A3 move into the corner, climbing up the left vertical wall then back to a ledge with bushes. The final pitch goes 15 feet horizontally left past a fixed piton, into the left wall, and up a groove to the summit. The six leads are rated as follows: 5.5; 5.6,A2; 5.7,A1; 5.7; 5.6,A3; 5.7. Descend via the Knife Edge or pick your way down, starting 100 feet to the west of the top of the route.

Route 12, Chicken Chop Suey, IV, 5.8. Ten pitches; this route is a variation of Procrastination. The first five pitches are the most difficult. The fourth lead is hard, sustained 5.8 climbing. Also, there is 5.7 or 5.8 climbing getting up off the ground on the first lead which is exposed for much of the pitch and relatively unprotected with nuts. Rock is good, particularly for the third and fourth leads, and only fair thereafter. This climb has been done both as a one- and two-day climb. If done in two days, the best bivouac is on a ledge at the top of the fourth pitch. This climb travels up the right side of the shallow rib on the Shield which can best be seen in the late afternoon.

Approach the base of the climb by scrambling up the ramp to the large shallow rib composed of three right-facing open books. About 150 feet down the ramp from the start of the Rainbow Route is a large boulder with an aspen growing between it and the face. Begin climbing a step or two down from the aspen. Climb unprotected for 15 feet (5.7) until it is possible to rest and place a nut, then begin a long traverse left with easier climbing but sparse protection with nuts. The traverse leads to a large, smooth ramp visible from below. Belay in a corner at the upper end of the ramp. From here, traverse left to a small corner, make an awkward move up, and follow the crack above to a belay at the top of a shattered ledge 120 feet above. At this point the climb begins its variation from Procrastination. The third pitch on Chicken Chop Suey follows the steep crack system directly above for two pitches of sustained 5.7 and 5.8 climbing. The crux is a squeeze chimney above a small roof on the fourth pitch. The fourth pitch ends at a large ledge which offers a spectacular view of the Rainbows to the right. Follow the obvious open book up from this point. The climb is the same as Procrastination for the remaining six pitches.

A good selection of nuts from small to very large is needed, as are numerous slings. Allow at least a full day.

Route 13, Pickle, III, 5.8. Five pitches including third class. Quality of rock is good. This climb starts from the upper large group of trees mentioned in the description for the Standard S Route. The climb can be reached either by climbing up on Route 4 or 5, or by doing one or two rappels down from the top (double rope) to reach the large group of trees.

By whatever means used to gain the large group of trees, begin the climb by walking left to a dihedral that is 50 feet past the big tree under the overhangs. Climb up onto somewhat loose blocks and traverse left to a corner, then up and right to a belay ledge. Next, third class 40 feet to a higher ledge and climb up and slightly right to a large flake which can be laybacked to a sparse belay at a horizontal crack under a roof. Step down and traverse 30 feet to the right almost to the corner where it is necessary to make several difficult (5.8) moves up. Easier climbing leads to a partial chimney which is followed to the ledge at its top for the next belay. The last lead goes 25 feet to the right then follows the obvious crack system to the top. Short, thick horizontal pitons were used to protect the crux on the first ascent.

Route 14, Interrupted Journey, IV, 5.7, A3. Eight pitches. Quality of rock is good. Start the climb near the top of the ramp and do one fourth-class pitch up an obvious crack and two 5.6 pitches which put you under a large roof. Difficult A3 climbing on small nuts, cliffhangers, and two fixed pitons allow you to turn the overhang. Easy rock above leads to the crux move; a hard 5.7 move around a bulge and overhang. Four pitches of 5.6 climbing in a large crystalline chimney to the right of a large dihedral complete the climb. Protection is good for this climb.

Route 15, Slipping into Darkness, IV, 5.8, A3. Eleven pitches. This climb is a variation of Procrastination. Quality of rock is good.

The first pitch for this route is the same as the first pitch on Chicken Chop Suey. The next pitch begins with a third-class traverse to the left. When the traverse begins to get more difficult, the route goes up and wanders around to a belay at a small tree 80 feet below the large dihedral (which is the object of the variation). The third lead continues up on easy rock left of the tree to the base of the dihedral, then 60 feet up the awkward crack in the dihedral to a hanging belay. The fourth pitch continues up the dihedral to the obvious overhang. Difficult (5.8) freeclimbing leads to the overhang which is turned by going from left to right (A2 or A3). The pitch ends on a small ledge 15 feet above the overhang. The fifth pitch starts on aid (A1) in the same crack system to gain a ledge ten feet above. Traverse left 40 feet at the ledge to exit the dihedral and gain easier rock. Run out the rope and belay. The sixth pitch involves easy climbing but has some rotten rock. Run out the rope to easy rock and third class up and right to the beginning of the sixth pitch of Procrastination and Chicken Chop Suey. This route has also been climbed free at 5.10.

The overhang on the fourth pitch can be climbed clean by using 1, 2, and 3 crack 'n' ups in addition to a normal nut selection. Other handy special equipment includes 8 and 9 titons. Protection is generally adequate but may be tricky to find. Rock varies from fair to good.

Route 16, Orange Sunshine, V, 5.9, A4. Nine pitches. Start this climb about 30 feet above the start of Procrastination and about 40 feet below the start of the Rainbow Route. The climb starts directly beneath a prominent right-facing and right-leaning dihedral that is about 30 feet off the ground. Easy climbing leads to the base of this open book which is climbed until about halfway up when it is feasible to make a short traverse left, out of the dihedral and into a trough. Follow the trough to a belay ledge which has bolts. From the ledge move up and left on fourth-class ledges that end in a crack that diagonals to the left. Go up the crack about 40 feet until you can leave it by way of a vertical crack system that runs out just below a large ledge at the bottom of a large bowl-shaped feature. From this ledge climb a distinct left-facing dihedral at the right side of the bowl and belay on a block at its top. The next pitch begins 15 feet up at the top of the next block, which also makes a good two-man bivouac location. The fourth pitch begins with a tension traverse left for 15 feet then up a shallow dihedral that deteriorates to loose flakes. Climb up and left across the flakes until you come to the right end of a square roof. Traverse left under the roof and turn its left end on aid, setting a hanging belay just around the corner. The next pitch goes left on a 15-foot tension traverse to a small dihedral that leads through the next roof. Climb through the roof then up a steep 50-foot head-wall to a huge ledge and belay. The route continues up the pinnacle to the left, staying on its inside corner until it is possible to belay. From here, a fourth-class pitch puts you on ledges that join with Chicken Chop Suey/ Procrastination. Three fourth-class pitches and one fifth class lead the rest of the way to the summit.

Route 17, Super Glide, IV, 5.8, A3. Quality of rock is good. Crux pitches are the fourth and sixth. Start at the base of a right-leaning, overhanging crack below a roof on the north end of the Shield. This crack has some dark stains in and below it along with some lime depos-its. Begin up the right leaning crack to a belay ledge with a bolt. Continue up a shattered pillar and belay at a bolt just below an overhang. The third pitch traverses into a dihedral and continues to the top of the dihedral and ends at belay pins on the right. The fourth pitch involves a tension traverse left to a bolt and continues up to a belay ledge in a dihedral 60 feet below a large roof. The next pitch goes up left to a bolt then traverses right to a belay at a fixed bong. The sixth pitch (A3) follows the crack between a large flake and a roof to the lip of the roof which requires an exciting mantle. Be-lay above at a bolt and continue to the top with easy freeclimbing.

Route 18, Cowboy's Delight, V, 5.9, A3. This is a varia-tion of Orange Sunshine, consisting of three short pitches. The variation starts on the left-hand side of the large ledges that are near the top of Orange Sunshine and directly beneath the obvious Cyclops overhangs. Climb a shattered crack system that leaves the upper left corner of the ledges and head for the base of the arching dihedral that can be seen above. Belay on a sloping slab at the beginning of the arch. Next, traverse to a thin, steep crack on the face next to the dihedral and follow to the arch. Climb the arch, turning the overhang at its peak and belay 20 feet farther at two bolts placed above a scrawny pine tree. Finish the climb by traversing left six feet to gain an open book that slants up and right to the summit. The three pitches are rated 5.9, 5.8/A3, and 5.9.

Route 19, Rainbow Dancer, V, 5.10+. At the base of the Rainbow Route are two large pine trees. Directly opposite the easternmost tree is a bush-filled crack which closes off 20 feet above the ground. Faceclimb up this crack until you can traverse right and then up to a two bolt belay. The second pitch goes up the left facing corner for 150 feet to another pair of bolts. From this belay climb up a crack past a fixed pin then up and left to another fixed pin. From the second piton traverse straight left 30 feet to a belay. The fourth pitch goes up and left to a right-facing corner at the right-hand end of the little Rainbow overhang. Follow this for 80 feet and belay. Traverse right on thin faceclimbing then right and up, to a belay beneath a small triangular roof. Pitch 6 turns the roof on the right then goes left up to a belay on a small ledge in a corner. The next lead goes up a spectacularly exposed flake at the left end of the ledge then up 30 feet to an airy traverse above overhangs. Climb up and left to a corner which is turned to the left 25 feet below a whitish roof, past a fixed piton, on to rounded holds (5.10+), and up to a hanging belay in a good crack left of the roof. The next pitch climbs the corner above and ends on a large, grassy ledge. Fom here climb up and right for two pitches to the top.

UNM Spire

This spire is just below the base of the ramp on the

UNM Spire. Photo by David Benyak.

Shield. Approach and descend by hiking up Juan Tabo Canyon or by the Fletcher Trail variation.

Route 1, Saddle Route, I, 5.3. One pitch. Quality of rock is poor. Begin at the saddle, between the spire and the lower face of the Shield, which is reached by scrambling up one of the gullies on either side of the spire. Climb up the northwest corner or slightly to the left on the north face.

Route 2, Standard South Ridge Route, II, 5.5. Five pitches. Quality of rock is fair to poor. Last three pitches are somewhat harder. Begin climb at the base of the south ridge. After three leads traverse onto the west face to avoid the obvious overhang. Follow the west face to the summit.

Route 3, Southwest Corner, II, 5.7. Four fifth-class pitches. Quality of rock is poor. Difficulty of climbing is fairly sustained throughout the climb. Begin the climb just east of the south ridge in a pocket of red, crumbly rock and climb 70 feet up a poorly protected slab, keeping just east of the ridge and ending at a small ledge below another slab. Continue up a hard-to-protect slab for 60 feet to a small ledge under some slightly over-hanging blocks. The third lead, 90 feet long, follows a ramp through the overhanging blocks then goes directly up a large slab to a ledge midway on the slab. From this ledge, the final pitch gains the south ridge at the end of the large slab and continues up the ridge through large loose blocks to the summit.

Route 4, East Face, I, 4. Follow a series of easy ledges up the east face to the summit. You will probably want a rope at least for the descent.

Route 5, West Face to South Ridge, II, 5.5. Five pitches. The last three pitches are the hardest. Quality of rock is fair. Begin climb by following a crack for one pitch up to a tree. Traverse left across a low-angle slab to a large ledge then continue traversing up on the next three pitches until you reach the summit.

The Prow

The Prow is the formation that somewhat resembles a fireplug and is located just west of the Needle. The Prow is a frequently climbed rock today and has been popular since early climbing activity in the Sandias. The first recorded ascent was in 1948 although the first ascent may actually have occurred earlier. Lightning has unfortunately destroyed some early register information and the earliest ascents may have gone unrecorded altogether. The Prow has long been a favorite for organized mountain club climbs, principally on the northwest and southeast ridges.

Approach by way of the Movie Trail. The trail leads to the base of the northwest ridge then skirts around the Prow to the south and back up to the saddle at the base of the southeast ridge. Standard descent routes are the southeast ridge and the northwest ridge. In descending the southeast ridge scramble down to a ledge where further progress is blocked. Fix a long sling around the large, rounded boulder at the east end of the ledge and perform one rappel, downclimbing the remainder. The other descent route at the northwest ridge involves two rappels. Rappel down to the east end of a broad ramp using a large dead tree as your first rappel anchor. Then walk down the ridge until further progress becomes difficult. Perform the second rappel off a large flake, ending up just south of the ridge proper. Two ropes are helpful when descending the northwest ridge.

Route 1, Southeast Ridge, I, 4. Two roped pitches. Quality of rock is fair to poor. The most difficult sections can be avoided by traversing left or right. This is the standard beginner route which follows the ridge proper to the summit. The worst part of the climb is the exhausting scramble up to the saddle at the base of the southeast ridge where the climb begins.

Route 2, South Face, I, 5.5. Three pitches. The second pitch is the most difficult. Quality of rock is fair to poor. The first pitch begins by climbing up to the east end of the long ramp that runs across the lower south face. Traverse to the west end of this ramp and belay. The second lead goes up a short face, keeping to the left (5.5) and up a small overhang (5.5) above the face. The third lead goes up a loose crack system and ends with scramble to the summit.

Route 3, Bird Ridge, II, 5.6 or 5.7. Four pitches. Quality of rock is fair to poor. Second and third leads are the most difficult. There is no one obvious route, but there are at least four variations up Bird Ridge. The climb generally begins at the base of the southwest ridge and proceeds up the ridge beside a large flake to a roomy ledge. From this ledge several variations can be followed ending up with a scramble to the top. One such variation is to climb straight up from the roomy ledge to an overhang and traverse left about 30 feet, then up to a small ledge where a belay is set. The third and fourth pitches then go directly up the obvious crack; the last pitch is a belayed scramble. Belay stances are often small but usually well protected. Watch for loose rock on the last two pitches.

Route 4, Northwest Ridge, I, 5.3. Two pitches. The second pitch is the more difficult. Follow the ridge along the obvious route, then scramble to the top.

Route 5, Hanging Sling Buttress, III, 5.8. Five pitches. Quality of rock is fair to poor. This climb is located on the southwest face of the Prow and begins about 100

The Prow. Photo by Rick Meleski.

feet to the right of the beginning of Bird Ridge. Climb about 75 feet to a belay point at the top of a right-facing dihedral. An old bolt is located at this point. Continue up and left to Roomy Ledge. Climb straight up from the right-hand side of Roomy Ledge to a long, horizontal ledge above and belay from the middle of this ledge. The next lead traverses to the right side of the ledge and climbs (5.7) past old slings and pitons to the top of a small buttress. Belay from the top of the buttress. The fourth pitch traverses (5.8) from the buttress to a vertical crack above an overhang. Climb the crack (5.7) until it begins to run out below a small overhang. Exit right and climb a series of small ledges to a good crack below a small overhang. Climb up through the overhang (5.6 or 5.7). One further fourth-class pitch leads to the summit.

Needle

The Needle is the impressive spire immediately south of the east end of the Shield. The Needle was originally called the Pyramid, which best describes its shape, and was the site of some of the earliest climbing in the local area. The earliest record of a first ascent was made in 1944. In all likelihood, however, the first true ascent probably occurred sometime during the 1930s. Most of the early ascents were via the East Saddle. A number of free solos are mentioned including one apparently done by author Edward Abbey on August 12, 1951.

For climbs on the south and east part of the Needle, approach by hiking one-half mile north of the crest radio towers and descending the limestone rim just south of a prominent bulge in the crest ridge. Hike down to the saddle at the east side of the Needle, and from the saddle, make your way to the base of the appropriate climb. For climbs on the west side approach by hiking

The Needle with the Prow in the foreground flanked by Juan Tabo Canyon on the left and Pinnacle Valley on the right. Photo by Mike Hill.

up the Movie Trail, skirting the Prow to the south, and scrambling up to the base of the Needle.

The huge ramp visible from the west is called Fifth Avenue. This ramp effectively divides the west face into an upper and a lower half, and provides either a beginning or an end for most of the routes on the west side. Fifth Avenue also provides an escape route, which is accomplished by walking around to the north and exiting just below the East Saddle. The Needle may be closed to climbing for several months of the summer because of historic protected species habitat. Check first with the Tijeras Forest Service Ranger Station.

Route 1, East Saddle, I, 4. Two or three pitches. Reach this climb by scrambling down to the East Saddle from the crest as described previously. Reach the summit after two leads of easy but exposed scrambling, climbing on either the north or the south side of the obvious buttress above the saddle. Watch for loose blocks on this climb.

Route 2, East Saddle Caves, I, 5.4. Three pitches. Quality of rock is good on the third lead, fair on the rest of the climb. Two large shelter caves are noticeable from a distance on the east face of the Needle, but impossible to see from below. This climb begins directly below the northernmost cave which is almost obscured by trees. The first lead is a roped scramble to the mouth of the cave. From the cave climb up to the right and traverse back left over the cave. The third lead is the hardest and travels directly up from the cave over rounded rock which is difficult to protect with nuts. The climb ends with a scramble to the summit.

Route 3, Southeast Ridge, II or III, 5.4. Five or six pitches of fifth-class climbing. Approach by scrambling down from the East Saddle, by hiking down the top part of the Chimney Canyon Trail and then north across Pinnacle Valley. The climbing route actually covers only the top part of the Southeast Ridge making it necessary to enter the ridge a little below midpoint. This is usually done by scrambling down the couloir south of the East Saddle, turning the base of the southeast ridge, and scrambling up the couloir that separates the southeast and southwest ridges. Scramble up into a huge bowl in the couloir. From the bowl, roped climbing leads to a number of entry points on the southeast ridge. The ridge is then followed up for two or three more leads until you reach a friction slab with a step near the top. Fifth-class climbing ends at this point and the climb becomes a scramble to the top.

If you climb the entire ridge, there are an additional six leads on the steep bottom third of the ridge. The difficulty of this section is 5.7 or 5.8 with some possible A1.

The Needle. Photo by David Benyak.

Route 4, Southwest Ridge, III, 5.7 or 5.8. Fifteen pitches. This is probably the longest climb of any difficulty in the Sandias. Allow a minimum of 12 hours of daylight for a strong party of two. Minimum actual climbing time is seven to eight hours. The difficulty is fairly sustained all the way up with some difficult 5.7 or 5.8 climbing. The many small variations available in the route affect the difficulty of the climb. Quality of rock is good. Approach the climb by hiking up the Movie Trail and past the Prow to the base of the southwest ridge. Another approach which is perhaps easier to accomplish, although harder to find, is to hike down the burned-out gully from the Cake-Candle overlook.

There are two basic beginnings to the southwest ridge route, one on the east side of the ridge and one on the west side. Neither is completely straightforward. However, both should bring you quickly and easily to a large square-sided trough with a very prominent central cave located about 40 feet above a large bushy ledge about 300 feet up the ridge. To start from the east, note that a prominent dark chimney is the east face of the ridge. One or two fourth-class pitches lead up and right to the foot of this chimney at which point one should turn left on an easy ledge to the ridgeline. Follow easy fifth-class cracks up and left to the ledge mentioned above. To begin the route from the west, look just west of the southernmost toe of the ridge to find a steep face with several arched overhangs above gentle bushy ledges. Scramble to the right side of these ledges, and begin easy fifth-class climbing up and somewhat left for about a pitch, at which point the cave above becomes visible. Follow cracks either along the ridge or up the trough face to the bushy ledge. From the ledge, climb steep cracks on either side of the trough to the right side of the cave and then up to another ledge. Three cracks above lead up

Jim Fuge on the southeast ridge of the Needle. Photo by Carl Smith.

the last 30 feet of the trough to easy ledges which drop down to the first notch in the ridge and complete the first four pitches of the climb. (This notch, or saddle, can be used to retreat from the climb by performing a 150-foot rappel down the east side.) The fifth lead involves difficult climbing up a crack system at the left side of the notch and is followed by an easy pitch which goes up a crack to the east side of the ridge. The seventh lead goes up a high-angle slab, over a broken area to the left of a pine tree and up a gully to the next belay.

The next pitch continues onto the ridge and goes fourth class to a small notch farther up the ridge. The ninth lead goes from the small notch west and across to a crack system which is followed by a traverse into a smooth, open chimney, above which is the next belay stance. Pitch ten moves onto the ridge and goes fourth class to the next large notch in the ridge. At this point, the south end of Fifth Avenue intersects the ridge and one can retreat by walking north along Fifth Avenue. This also provides a handy ledge on which to lunch or bivouac.

The eleventh pitch proceeds up from the notch to a chimney and the following pitch proceeds on up the face and to the east of the ridge. Continue on the next lead up a short crack to a large ledge with an old tree on top. Pitch 14 goes up a crack behind the tree and the following pitch continues up the crack system and ends with a fourth-class scramble to a belay spot. Scramble or fourth class the rest of the way to the top.

Route 5, II, 5.7, A1. Up to six pitches to Fifth Avenue. This climb starts up a large shallow chimney, or steep couloir, which appears in the center of the lower west face of the Needle when viewed from Albuquerque. Third class up the chimney until it starts to get vertical then do a short easy pitch up and left to a ledge with a large tree. Aid the face above the tree utilizing an old bolt and finish the pitch on a ledge above. The next pitch goes left around the corner and involves an unprotected layback (5.7) above a large ledge. Finish with easy climbing to Fifth Avenue. Overall quality of rock is fair.

Route 6, Hoy's Chimney, I, 5.4. Two pitches. The route is located in the deep chimney that connects the lower west face, just north of midface, to Fifth Avenue. The first 100 feet is fourth class or easy fifth class and leads to a water seepage area which is slippery and poorly protected. Above the seepage is a scramble up to one last friction slab just below Fifth Avenue. This friction slab is the crux. An alternate route can be climbed just to the left of Hoy's Chimney in one lead. It goes 5.3 but the rock is very loose. Descend via a rappel down a couloir just to the right of the main route or continue up to the top of the Needle by way of Route 8.

Route 7, Northwest Ridge, II, 5.7. Three pitches. Begin the climb about 100 feet south of the base of the northwest ridge. Climb two leads to an overhang. Move around the overhang to the north and ascend a small face that is the crux of the climb. Two fixed pitons are located on the face. Just above the difficult face are some friction slabs that mark the end of the fifth class climbing. Some trees just above the friction slabs lead to Fifth Avenue. The ridge above Fifth Avenue is third class to the top.

Route 8, Upper West Face Direct, II; 5.5. Five pitches. Reach this climb by hiking up past the Prow and then by scrambling up from the saddle between the Prow and the Needle to Fifth Avenue. The climb begins on Fifth Avenue up a large gully in the center of the upper west face, just above Hoy's Chimney. After the initial section, easy climbing leads up a final small face to the north of an outcropping and on to the top. One can descend by rappelling down to Fifth Avenue or by descending the East Saddle. Hiking time to reach the base of the climb is about two hours.

Route 9, Upper West Face Variation, II, 5.5. Five pitches. The bottom part of this route is the same as for Route 8. After the first third of the climb, angle to the right over easy ledges which join the upper section of the southwest ridge.

Hidden Wall

Hidden Wall is the large wall immediately to the east of the Needle. Reach the wall by scrambling down from the East Saddle of the Needle. Several 5.7 to 5.8 climbs have been done on Hidden Wall, but no detailed route information is presently available.

Pinnacle Valley

Pinnacle Valley is just south of the Needle. In 1967 a forest fire swept up this valley and the remains of the fire are still evident. The Tombstone is the most prominent rock formation in the valley; however, many small spires and pinnacles are located in the upper part. Some of these such as the Knifeblade immediately south of the Tombstone, and the Pillar, a 40-foot block located on the wall west of the Knifeblade, have been climbed, but little route information is available. A number of these formations, most unnamed, would provide enjoyable short climbs.

Tombstone

This aptly named structure dominates the upper end

of Pinnacle Valley. It is reached by dropping down from the Crest Trail approximately ¼ mile north of the radio towers. From the Crest Trail the east side of the Tombstone appears as a flat ramp. Descend the Tombstone by scrambling down the east side.

Route 1, West Face Traverse, I, 5.5. Two pitches. This is the standard west face route. The first pitch is probably the more difficult. Quality of rock is excellent on the first pitch but only fair on the second pitch. The climb starts up a deceptive-looking crack on the southwest ridge. From the top of the crack traverse all the way across to the north end of the obvious ledge which lies halfway up the west face. The second lead then angles back up to the right and ends at the summit. The second pitch can be made harder by starting up the northwest ridge instead of staying on the face.

Route 2, North Face, II, 5.9. Two pitches. Quality of rock is fair to good. Climb the prominent series of cracks running up the center of the north face. You encounter the crux about 70 feet up the first pitch in the form of a three-inch crack (5.8 or 5.9). Belay above the first large overhang. There is loose rock on the second lead. A 1½-inch angle is fixed on the first lead. Hardware carried for this climb should include a selection of large nuts and many slings.

Route 3, West Face-Left Side, I, 5.8. Two pitches. Begin the climb about 25 feet from the north end of the west face, atop a small flake separated from the face. Face-climb about 20 feet until you reach a 1½-inch crack. Layback and jam (5.8) up past several bulges and a bush until you reach the main horizontal ledge which splits the face. Belay from the far left of the ledge. Continue up within 20 feet of the north corner to the top.

Route 4, West Face Direct, I, 5.7 or 5.8. Two pitches. Quality rock is good. Begin the climb at the top of a 30-

foot buttress located 20 or 30 feet north of the southwest corner (Route 1). Belay from two bolts. Face climb until you reach a crack and follow this until you come to the broad ledge halfway up the face. From the ledge continue up to a narrow chimney and face climb (in a bushy dihedral) to the top. Difficulty is about equal for each lead.

Route 5, Feats Don't Fail Me Now, II, 5.10. Two pitches. This climb apparently begins up the same crack system mentioned in the description for Route 2.

Begin the climb up the crack which lies in the center of the face. Start in a right-facing corner off a ledge and under a large overhang. Climb to the overhang, turning it to the left. Continue up steep face and cracks to a second overhang which is turned at the right end. Above the second overhang, traverse right and climb a corner to the top of a pedestal. Steep face and lieback climbing lead up from the pedestal to a V notch where a belay is set. The second lead goes up the right-hand crack out of the notch to a large ledge. From the ledge climb a short but steep face and crack system which leads to the ridge just below the summit.

Knifeblade

This is the blade-like formation which sits just south and slightly east of the Tombstone.

Route 1, Crack of Black, I, 5.8. Two pitches. This route is on the west face of the Knifeblade; it goes up through the black lichen that abounds on the entire climb. Climb up to a small overhang (5.8) using a bolt for protection. Diagonal right for 50 feet until you reach a notch in the face. The second pitch is in a continuous 1½-inch crack which runs to the top of the face (5.8). Rappel back down the climbing route to descend.

The Tombstone. Photo by David Benyak.

Mummy

The Mummy is located in, appropriately enough, Mummy Canyon, just to the south of Pinnacle Valley. The Mummy is a 50-foot spire on the south rim of the lower part of the canyon. It is best approached by hiking down the upper part of the Chimney Canyon Trail (see approach to the Chimney) and then cutting to the north of "CC" Couloir which is located at the north end of the aspen meadow below the limestone bands.

Route 1, I, A2. One pitch. Start at the southeast corner and climb up the south face and over a small bulge just below the summit. Several pitons are still in place and a bolt is placed near the top. Also a bolt has been placed on the summit as a rappel anchor. Nuts are better for aid than the pitons originally used on this climb.

Castle

The Castle is the large rib located at the north end of the series of walls and formations which includes Muralla Grande, the Cake, the Candle, and the Lookout. It is at the lower north side of "CC" Couloir and is separated from the crest proper by a couloir. Approach by going above and to the north of "CC" Couloir as if going to the Mummy. Upon reaching upper Mummy Canyon, drop several hundred feet down into the canyon and traverse west along the south side of the canyon until you reach the ridge overlooking the east face of the Castle. Alternately, approach by hiking down the top part of Chimney Canyon and then hiking north past Muralla Grande.

Route 1, Upper South Ridge, II, 5.5, A2 or 5.10. Begin the climb by scrambling up to the notch on the middle west face. Climb to the south up a 50-foot face to a

The Mummy. Photo by David Benyak.

grassy ramp. Then traverse toward the south ridge and climb up a steep gully which ends on a prominent ledge on the south ridge. Continue up the south ridge using a steep aid pitch which ends with an escape to the right. Continue up a gully to a good belay spot. An easy lead ends on the lower of the two summits. The true summit is a short fifth-class lead from the summit notch.

Route 2, Crujida Reina, II, 5.9. Two pitches. The climb begins on the smooth lower south face of the Castle. Third class to a flat ledge beneath a very prominent jam-crack. The first pitch goes up the jamcrack (the beginning is somewhat vague) to a stance in an alcove beneath a chimney. The next pitch goes up the crack to its top. From the top of the crack one can continue up the south ridge to the summit as in Route 1, or do a 160-foot rappel to reach the bottom of the climb. If this climb is combined with Route 1 to reach the summit, the grade should be increased to III.

Route 3, Nada Wall, I, 5.7, A1 or A2. One pitch. On the ridgeline down from and due west of the Castle is a very distinct small blank wall. The route starts beneath the middle of the face. Climb a small right-facing open book that ends on a ledge with a large bush on it. From the extreme right side of the ledge a skyhook move gets you to a bolt-bathook ladder which you follow to a small crack that breaks the very top of the smooth face in its middle. Descend by way of a 70-foot rappel.

In addition to a selection of nuts, bring ¼-inch bolt hangers and bathooks for the climb.

Route 4, Crujida Puta, III, 5.9, A1. Climb the first pitch of Crujida Reina. Traverse right on hooks and free for about 20 feet to next crack. Climb this until even with a small pine tree that should be to your left. Traverse to the tree (hooks) and climb the nice crack above the tree

The Castle. Photo by David Benyak.

to the ledges above. Continue via the old route to the summit or rappel as in Crujida Reina.

El Tecolote

El Tecolote is the face behind the Castle. Approach via the ridge on the south side of Mummy Canyon then descend behind the Castle.

Route 1, Quack, III, 5.9. Four pitches. Descending the gully behind the Castle is an obvious bush-filled dihedral with a clean crack 50 feet to the left. Third class up to within 15 feet of the start of the crack then rope up to gain a belay ledge 15 feet higher up. The next two pitches involve sustained climbing up the crack to a hanging belay 15 feet below an alcove. From here, go left 10 feet then up to the top.

Route 2, Crystal Corner, III, 5.9. Four pitches. Start up a crack at the bottom of a large dihedral and belay. Continue up the right wall of the dihedral and belay to the right at a small tree. Traverse left from the tree and continue up the right face of the dihedral. The final pitch continues up, finishing on easier ground.

Cake

This is a large rib which is located at the north end of and just west of Muralla Grande. It derives its name from the overhanging bulge, located near the top (opposite the Candle) which resembles a slice of cake. It is connected to Muralla Grande by a well-defined saddle on which sits the Candle, an unmistakable spire. The Candle is about 35 feet east of the Cake and the two formations are often used to rig a Tyrolean traverse. Both the Cake and the Candle are approached via "CC"

Couloir. This couloir is located just below and to the north of the aspen meadow mentioned in the approach to the Chimney. It is a small, steep couloir which can be best descended by keeping to the north side. A rope is sometimes used to gain the notch between the Cake and the Candle.

Route 1, North Face, I, 5.3. Two pitches. Quality of rock is good. Begin the climb from the notch between the Cake and the Candle. Climb up a diagonal chimney to a ledge which you follow across the north face to the northwest ridge. This ridge is then followed to the summit via an easy layback crack which is the crux of the climb. Rappel (double rope) down the north face to descend.

Route 2, West Face Traverse, I, 5.4. Two pitches. This route is a variation of Route 1. The variation begins at the point where Route 1 intersects the northwest ridge. From the northwest ridge, traverse across the west face to the south ridge, and then follow the south ridge to the summit.

Route 3, Corkscrew, I, 5.5. Rappel down "CC" Couloir to the base of the west face of the Cake where the climb begins. Scramble up broken ledges on the right and then go left up a 70-foot gully. Angle right to the south ridge. Then go around the ridge corner and across the wide but tricky ledges below the upper east face to the notch separating the Cake and the Candle. Finish by way of the North Face Route.

Route 4, South Couloir, I, 5.2. One pitch of fifth-class climbing. Although this climb is easy the approach is long. Approach from Chimney Canyon up the long gully that separates the Cake from Muralla Grande. Scramble up the couloir until you come to a 50-foot wide bowl several hundred feet up. One roped lead is sufficient to ascend the bowl, and the rest of the climb is a scramble up to the notch between the Cake and the Candle.

Route 5, A Piece of Cake, I, A3, 5.8. One lead. This route is primarily aid. Drop down from the notch between the Cake and the Candle to a crack which goes up the slightly overhanging south face of the Cake. Aid up the crack to a bolt which protects a short section of freeclimbing which leads to the top. Recommended equipment: nuts, thin pitons, and a bathook.

Candle

See discussion for Cake.

Route 1, Southeast Corner, I, 5.5. One pitch. Quality of rock is good. Begin in the notch separating the Cake from the Candle. Traverse across the south face to the southeast corner, which is very exposed, and continue up the corner. After about 20 feet start bearing back to the left until forced to mantle (or wallow) into a recess which gains the summit. This mantle (5.5+) is the crux of the climb. Two pitons are placed on top as a rappel anchor. Rappel down to the notch between the Cake and the Candle.

Route 2, West Face Direct, I, A2(?). Start from the northwest corner and freeclimb 15 feet up a steep crack which veers toward the center of the face. Direct aid is used for the remainder of the climb. The crack continues up to a small ledge halfway up the face. The rotten crack on the left side of the ledge leads to the summit.

Route 3, West Face Escape, I, A2, 5.4 (?). Climb the west face as described in Route 2. However, when you reach the small halfway ledge, traverse over onto the south face. Angle up to the southeast corner, perform a mantle, and proceed to the summit.

Route 4, North Face, I, A3, 5.6. Begin by freeclimbing

Tyrolean traverse between the Cake and the Candle. Photo by Bob Kyrlach.

up the roofed dihedral on the right side of the face. Aid climbing begins as you move right from under the roof and continue up, angling left on an obvious series of cracks. You must then aid several small bulges above the top of these cracks; the final section to the summit is done free.

Muralla Grande

Muralla Grande is a massive face east of the Cake and north of the Chimney. The easiest approach for most of the wall is probably that described for the Chimney. When you reach the base of the steep couloir that leads to the Chimney, make your way north along the base of Muralla Grande. The top of Muralla Grande is just west of the aspen meadow area at the top of the steep couloir north of the Chimney. A nice vantage point for viewing Muralla Grande is atop the "front porch," a platform at the top of a small rib immediately west from the center of the wall. Relatively limited climbing has been done on Muralla Grande considering its size and possibilities.

Route 1, La Selva Route, III, 5.7. Five or six pitches. There is frequent 5.7 climbing but little sustained climbing of this difficulty. Quality of rock is fair but beware of large, loose blocks. Begin the climb at the center of the wall directly east and a little north of the front porch. The first pitch starts up a nice 40-foot, left-facing dihedral. From its top, gingerly pick your way through a more decomposed section of pinkish rock and belay at the base of a long, bushy dihedral which angles up and left. Climb and bushwhack the dihedral for two full pitches to an obvious medium-sized pine near the left edge of the main wall. There is a good ledge at this spot. The crux lead goes straight up a few feet right of the tree for 45 feet of difficult 5.7 climbing. From here the diffi-

route hidden
by wall

dotted line indicates
optional routes

route begins on other
side of buttress

*Muralla Grande. Photo by
David Benyak.*

culty eases and two more leads of easy climbing lead to the top.

Route 2, *Clark's Cramps*, III, 5.8. Five pitches. Quality of rock is fair to good. Begin the climb to the right of a large buttress in a large right-facing corner. (The same start can be used as for Routes 4 and 8.) Two fifth-class pitches with some 5.7 climbing lead to easier rock and then to a large grassy ledge in the center of the face just above and to the right of the large central overhangs— called Football Ledge because of its spaciousness. From the upper left end of Football Ledge follow a crack to a short overhanging crack (5.8) which may be avoided by a short but tricky traverse to the right below the overhang. Two more pitches (some 5.7) lead to the top. A 5.7 variation exists from Football Ledge. To the right of the normal route is an obvious left-facing dihedral which you can follow for two to three pitches (some 5.7) to the top.

Route 3, *Labor Day Route*, III, 5.5. Eight pitches. The harder leads are near the top with the remainder of the climb being low fifth class in difficulty. Quality of rock on the first few leads is fair but improves on the upper half of the climb. The route starts near the north end of the face and progresses gradually south and up. It ends near the center of the west face north of the large cleft in the face wall.

Route 4, *Warpy Moople*, III, 5.9. Eight pitches. This route has some of the cleanest and most solid crack and faceclimbing in the Sandias. The climb starts directly beneath the large overhangs located near the center of the wall. Begin climbing in a dihedral up and to the left of a tree. At the end of the dihedral move left and up to loose blocks leading to a small dirt ledge. From the ledge move left through some bushes to a right-arching crack. From the end of this crack traverse right and then

Paul Horak on the crux pitch of Warpy Moople. Photo by Andrew Emrick.

diagonal right to a grass-lumped ledge beneath a small overhang. Traverse right above the overhang and then up to a belay ledge at the right of and below the large overhang. Next, go straight up very solid rock to a ledge beneath a bulge. From the left end of the ledge go up and then traverse right above the bulge to an open book which you follow until it ends. From this point traverse right onto the face and then up to a move (protected by a fixed pin) which leads to a small ledge at the base of a crack system. The last two leads follow the crack systems farthest to the left.

Route 5, Short But Thin, III, 5.8. Seven pitches. Quality of rock is good. Begin the climb directly below the right end of the large overhangs which are located near the center of the face. Ascend a corner for 25 feet then exit right onto loose blocks. Mount the blocks and climb the face above. The faceclimbing continues for two and a half more pitches of moderate difficulty to the top of the third pitch, about 20 feet below and to the right of the large overhangs. Next traverse about 60 feet to the right on a ledge and set a belay. Ascend an easy face above this belay to the crux (5.8+) and continue another 30 feet to a big, grassy ledge. Finally, ascend a corner to the top or climb one pitch up the face to the right. Recommended nuts: stoppers 1 through 8 and hexcentrics 1 through 9.

Route 6, Masochist Variant, III, 5.9. Six pitches. This variation begins left of the large buttress which has as its summit the previously mentioned Football Ledge (see Clark's Cramps). The first pitch goes up then angles to the right across easy slabs. The second lead goes up then right to a bushy 40-foot left-facing corner, and ends on a good ledge to the right. Beware of loose rock on this pitch. Begin the third lead up an ominous left-facing corner (almost a chimney) to a roof 50 feet above. Turn the roof to the right (5.9) and follow easier climbing above to a broken area just below Football Ledge. From Football Ledge follow Clark's Cramps to the top.

Route 7, Fantasia, III, 5.8. Five pitches. Moderately sustained climbing. Quality of rock is poor to good. The climb begins about 200 feet north of a sharp-cornered dihedral which leads to a roof. Third class about 100 feet up a large bulge at the base of the face and set up a belay at the top of the bulge near an old piton-sling rappel anchor. The first pitch scrambles up and right on easy slabs to a smaller bulge. The second lead goes right, around a small overhang, and on to the opposite side of a small amphitheatre. Climb up 20 feet to a short wall then up to fractured rock and belay. The third lead goes up over small ledges and up the base of a large gully which runs diagonally up the face from south to north.

Scramble the full length of the gully to its highest point (on Football Ledge) and belay. The next lead goes up over several overhangs to a large horizontal ledge. Walk straight across the ledge and climb up a shallow crack system. Climb a difficult (5.8) unprotected 15-foot dihedral. Continue up for 50 feet then right from the top of the dihedral and traverse right until a belay can be made. The last lead climbs straight up to the summit.

Route 8, Out to Lunch—Direct Variation, III, 5.10. Seven pitches. This climb follows Warpy Moople for the first two pitches. The third lead goes up mostly left 100 feet to a belay in a small niche below a small roof. Climb up and right through several small roofs and belay on a good ledge. The crux (5.10) occurs just above a bolt where a three-foot roof must be climbed. The next pitch (165 feet) follows the shallow dihedral directly above, past a fixed pin, then makes its way up to a belay stance formed by a large flake. Continue up the corner above 40 feet to a slanting roof (5.10) and belay just above. A final 5.7 pitch leads to the top.

Route 9, The Second Coming, II, 5.8. Four pitches. This climb is located on the south end of Muralla Grande, partially facing the Chimney. Locate the obvious steep headwall with three prominent vertical cracks. The climb begins below the right-hand crack and follows crack systems up for three pitches to a ledge below the right-hand crack of the previously mentioned three. The final pitch ascends this crack.

Route 10, Bunghole Borer, II, 5.9. Two pitches. This route is a variation of Second Coming. Climb the first two pitches of Second Coming. Climb up and a little left onto the steep face to a bulge halfway up the face. Traverse right then up into the dihedral on Second Coming and belay at the top of the dihedral. From here, traverse left 40 feet over easy rock to a fractured pillar, then up

Dan Roberts on Second Coming. Photo by Doug Bridgers.

and into the crack on the steep face. Continue up the few feet then right, into another crack system. Follow this crack to the top.

Route II, Dire Straights, II, 5.10. Rock is excellent. Protection is good. Climb the first two pitches of La Selva after which you should be under the large shallow dihedral left of the main roof system on the face. Climb straight up for 30 feet, then hand traverse left and past two small ledge systems. Follow a thin crack up until it ends, then traverse right and up into the large shallow dihedral and belay above a small roof to the right at a bolt. The fourth, or crux, pitch continues back up the dihedral to a fixed pin then traverse left and up. Climb through the roofs, step left, and belay at a fixed pin. The next pitch makes its way up the face and rejoins La Selva. Take along small wired stoppers through #10 hex.

Route 12, After Lunch, III, 5.10. Walk around the corner from Second Coming and locate a dead tree with a large flake lying against the rock. Climb the flake and the face above to a belay below a small roof. Go around the corner and up a crack (5.10) to Football Ledge. Move up a gully until in the middle of the face above the ledge and climb the face to a pedestal about 40 feet off the ledge. Continue up two more pitches of faceclimbing to the top.

Lookout

This rib is located on the north side of Chimney Canyon just below and west of the Cake. Approach is the same as that for Muralla Grande. Hiking time down is about ¾ hour; time back up is 1 to 1½ hours. Descend the summit of Lookout by rappelling down the northeast face from the north ridge.

Route 1, South Ridge, II, 5.7. Six or seven pitches. Quality of rock is fair. The climb starts at the bottom of the gully on the lower east side of the Lookout. Proceed up the most prominent southeast gully until blocked by a fir tree and traverse right to the base of the first pitch. Two and a half leads of easy climbing lead to a 50-foot 5.7 wall. Start at the left side of the wall and traverse diagonally to the east to a corner by a small tree. If this wall is aided, the climb goes 5.5, A1. Proceed up the ridge and continue up on the left of a west face to a belay position. Step across the exposed gully below and to the west of a belaying block. Traverse down and to the left of a crack running up the face to the right. Proceed up the crack to the next belay point. From here make a difficult move left to a crack and proceed up and over the next face. Complete the climb with a fingertip traverse to the summit.

Route 2, North Ridge. This climb begins at the base of "CC" Couloir and was first done in about 1967. No details about the route are available.

Chimney

The Chimney is a 150-foot spire located squarely in the center of the upper end of Chimney Canyon. To approach the Chimney, drive to the last cluster of buildings at the north end of the radio towers along the crest. Just west from these buildings a trail winds its way down through the limestone barrier. This is the upper part of one of the old La Luz trails which continues on down through Chimney Canyon (see Chimney Canyon Trail) and rejoins the present La Luz Trail near the mouth of the canyon. Follow the trail down from the crest until you reach a grove of aspen trees. From the aspen grove bear south and descend the steep couloir. The spire located just beyond the base of this approach couloir is the Chimney. The large wall just to the north of the Chimney is part of Muralla Grande. To descend the Chimney make one rappel down the east face off the large platform just below the summit.

Route 1, East Ridge, I, A1. Two pitches. Quality of rock is good. From the east notch climb up a crack system on the right side of the ridge until you reach a sizable platform shortly below the summit. Follow the obvious crack up from the platform to gain the summit.

Route 2, North Face Traverse, I, 5.4. Two pitches. Quality of rock is good. From the East Notch, traverse on the obvious ramp across the upper north face to a deep chimney which angles up and to the left, and ends at a platform just below the summit. From this platform, follow the obvious crack to the summit as in Route 1.

Route 3, West Side, II, A2, 5.7(?). The first two leads of this climb start from the base of the west ridge. Climb to a small ledge and then traverse around a corner and up to a sharp notch topped by several blocks. The remainder of the climb goes up the north face on aid and then around to the west face. From the notch, an overhang gives way to a crack system which leads to the bottom of the north face chimney. From here, traverse right and step around the northwest corner to the west face. Angle to the right up the west face and finish via the west side of the summit block crack.

Route 4, Notch to Upper West Face, I, 5.5. Two pitches. Quality of rock is good. Begin at East Saddle and traverse left, then up to the platform just east of and below the summit block. Climb the obvious crack to the top.

Route 5, Rocky Raccoon, I, 5.7. Two pitches. Both pitches are of similar difficulty. Quality of rock is good except for one or two loose blocks on the first pitch. This climb is the west variation of Route 6. Begin the climb adjacent to the dead tree at the base of the north face. Climb up keeping generally to the left. The crux of the first pitch occurs about 80 feet up when a sharp flake just to the right of a small overhang must be negotiated, followed by a wider crack on up above. Traverse left from the top of the difficult section into a deep notch blocked by a chimney. Set a belay either in the notch or continue on up to the left to the large ramp just above. The second lead continues straight up into a deep chimney which ends with any overhanging block about 15 feet up from the ramp. Move up around this block keeping to the right until you reach the large platform just below the summit. Finish via the obvious crack mentioned in Routes 1 and 2. Protection on this climb is excellent all the way up.

Route 6, North Face Direct, I, 5.7. Two pitches. The second pitch is the more difficult with the first pitch rated about 5.5. Quality of rock is good. Begin the climb up an obvious crack about 20 feet to the left of the dead tree which marks the start of Route 5. Continue up for about 100 feet, passing a fixed pin along the way, until forced to traverse 10 feet to the right into the deep notch mentioned in Route 5. Continue on to the ramp above and complete the climb as described in Route 5.

If the large chimney above the ramp appears too difficult, the second pitch can continue west along the ramp and ascend the standard North Face Chimney of Route 2. This reduces the overall difficulty of the climb to 5.5.

Route 7, Another Imbecile Variant, II, A3, 5.8. Three pitches. This route consists of three short leads which go up the west face and generally stay to the right of Route 3, coinciding near the top. Begin by aiding up a thin crack which leads to a hanging belay beneath a small roof. Pass the roof and then diagonal left to free-climbing which leads to a chimney which is followed to the top. Take along nuts, thin pitons, and a bathook.

Route 8, Schum's Delight, I, 5.9. Start up a crack (5.5) in the open book on the west side of the Chimney. Move up on to the block which is at the top of the lower northwest ridge and belay from here. Step across the notch from the block and proceed up the face to overhang. Move up to the right by jamming up the crack running down through the overhang (5.9) and proceed up a crack to a belay point on a ledge. Move above the ledge and traverse right to the ridge. Move off the ridge to the south and up to a crack which leads to the summit block.

This climb begins the same as Route 3 but varies to the right at the crux overhang.

Sentinel

The Sentinel is the prominent pinnacle which stands

on the upper south rim of Chimney Canyon. Reach the Sentinel by hiking directly down from the north end of the chain link fence that runs in front of the crest observation point to a limestone band at which point the Sentinel appears as a small rock pile to the northwest. Downclimb the limestone band and make your way down the ridge which lies between Chimney Canyon and upper La Cueva Canyon. Hike north of the notch at the east side of the Sentinel in order to gain the west side. Hiking time down to the Sentinel is about ½ hour. Descent from the summit of the Sentinel is accomplished by way of a short scramble down the east side.

Route 1, West Face, I, 5.5 or 5.6. Two pitches. This route starts just below the West Saddle on the north slope. Two cracks, three feet apart, mark the bottom of the route. Climb up the left crack for 20 feet (it plays out farther up) and continue up the right crack to a large belay ledge at the end of the first lead. Then angle right to avoid a series of overhangs on the left and traverse right on a small ledge to a crack which leads to the summit.

Route 2, Lost Ledge, I, 5.6. Two pitches. First pitch is the more difficult. Quality of rock is good. Begin the climb just to the right of the West Saddle and climb up the obvious smooth-faced dihedral which leads up the west end of the southwest face. Near the top of the dihedral traverse left out of the dihedral onto easier rock and make your way up to a belay stance. A final short, easy gully leads to the top. A variation is to follow the dihedral on up directly instead of traversing. This goes about 5.7 or 5.8. With a 165-foot rope this climb can be accomplished in one pitch. Protection is excellent.

Route 3, North Ridge, I, 5.7. Three pitches. Start on the northwest side of the Sentinel up a 5.6 open book, then proceed 30 feet beyond this to a belay point. Continue up the north ridge for 40 feet and traverse right to the base of a large crack. Proceed up the crack, which goes perhaps 5.7. The final pitch is a fourth-class scramble to the top.

Lower La Cueva Canyon

La Cueva Canyon is the major canyon which provides the traditional path up the west side of the Sandias. The present La Luz Trail follows upper La Cueva Canyon but its broad switchbacks avoid the lower part of the canyon. Lower La Cueva Canyon, however, provides the most direct access to some climbs in the Sandias, and in addition contains some short climbs of its own. These climbs are reached by hiking up La Cueva Canyon from La Cueva Picnic Grounds (see the description for La Cueva Trail in the hiking section). Short climbs are located on both sides of the canyon.

Route 1, The Incher, I, 5.9. One pitch. Just before reaching the water-streaked slabs on the right side of the lower canyon, walk up left and scramble to a rock near the ridge with an overhang having four consecutive vertical cracks. The Incher lies in the leftmost of these cracks. Climb up a friction ramp to a steep, flared 15-foot dihedral with a thin crack in it. Climb the dihedral (5.9) then follow the obvious crack through the double overhangs (5.9). The flared dihedral may be avoided by climbing either to the right (5.6) or the left (5.4) above the friction ramp.

Route 2, Gemstone, I, 5.8. Two pitches. Quality of rock is excellent. Difficulty is reasonably sustained. Gemstone is an obscure little rock on the south side of lower La Cueva Canyon. Reach this climb by hiking up La Cueva Canyon. Hike past the Bathtub Falls and look for the rocky ridge on the south side of the canyon. Just past this ridge is a dome-like formation of rock slabs. Gemstone is recognized by its left-facing dihedral with an arching overhang near the bottom. The arch of the overhang is steeple-shaped. Scramble up the side of the canyon to the overhang. Climb up a fairly large crack to the right of a dome-like bulge then traverse left a few feet and continue up the dihedral to a rocky belay ledge. From the right side of the ledge climb up a much smaller dihedral (5.7 or 5.8) which slopes up and to the left for 15 feet to a small ledge. Climb out and around a bush, then up to a small overhang. Surmount the overhang with the help of a small chockstone and continue on up the dihedral to the left. Descend by downclimbing (or rappelling) down rock to the right.

Route 3, *Markingstone*, I, 5.7, A2. One pitch. This climb is a variation to Gemstone. Climb the Gemstone squeeze chimney, then instead of traversing left under the slanting roof, climb up the roof on good wired nuts. Above, the face is a lower angle and the route follows a long, clean jamcrack to the top of the first pitch of Gemstone.

Route 4, *Seamingly Hard*, I, 5.10. Two pitches. Excellent rock. This climb is located on the smooth face immediately left of Gemstone. From the base of Gemstone climb up and left along a seam forming a shallow corner. Traverse right, past a bolt, to the belay ledge above the first pitch of Gemstone. The next lead goes up and left off a horn, past a bolt to a seam, then up the seam to a good crack 30 feet above the bolt. Finish the climb up the crack and belay to the left atop a boulder. Recommended equipment includes a selection with RP nuts.

Route 5, *Birthday Cake*, I, 5.10. Two pitches. This route is located along the descent route of Gemstone about 100 yards to the right of Gemstone. Begin by bushwhacking 50 feet up to an hourglass-shaped boulder with a crack running up its middle. Climb atop a block then up a thin crack until it ends and continue up past a flake to a small belay ledge. Continue up a crack, past a tree, and up a short, right-facing dihedral to steep rock on the right. Turn an overhang by the vertical crack above and belay.

Pulpit

The Pulpit is the first major pinnacle on the north side of La Cueva Canyon you reach while traveling up the La Luz Trail. It is directly east of Vista Point and generally marks the entrance to upper La Cueva Canyon. Approach the Pulpit by hiking up the La Luz Trail. Descend by way of a rappel off the back side. Two ropes are handy. Complete the descent by scrambling down the gully to the north to gain the trail.

Route 1, Southeast Ridge, II, 5.2. Four or five pitches. Begin the climb at the base of the southeast ridge immediately north of the La Luz Trail. The climb proceeds directly up the ridge on predominantly fourth-class rock. Make your way to the summit by climbing the large chimney located on the upper part of the ridge.

Route 2, Cave Route, II, 5.7. Four pitches. Begin by scrambling up to a dirt ledge directly below the prominent cave on the west face and climb up and to the right on a left-facing crack system. Belay on a blocky ledge. The next pitch traverses north for 10 feet then up to a large ledge with two bolts, just to the right of the cave. The third (crux) pitch starts with a difficult move off the south end of the ledge and continues up a crack system. A tricky traverse to the left leads up over broken rock to a belay at the base of a dihedral. The final pitch continues up the dihedral and up over easy but loose rock to the summit ridge; as an alternative, you can use a cleaner crack system to the right to finish the climb.

A direct variation (5.8) for reaching the cave is to begin the climb just left of the standard start in an obvious crack and up between two overhangs to a ledge above where the first belay is set. The second pitch goes directly up to the cave and coincides thereafter with the standard route.

Route 3, Waterstains, II, 5.7+. Four pitches. Start 50 feet left of the large right-leaning and overhanging arch on the south end of the west face in an open book which leads to a 6-foot overhang 125 feet above the ground. Climb the book staying to its right side until it is possible to traverse left past a fixed piton beneath the roof (5.7+) and faceclimb past the roof to its left side and up to a roomy ledge with bolts. From here make a long traverse right and follow the waterstains above to the top. This pitch does not protect well. A short scramble leads to the top.

Route 4, Poontang, III, 5.10. Three pitches. Hike up the La Luz Trail to a location opposite Vista Point directly below the southwest face of the Pulpit. Proceed to the aspen trees at the base of the rock. From here, a short gully up and left puts you on a flat ledge with a pine tree which marks the start of the climb. Begin up and left to a ledge. Continue on a crack slanting up and right until it is possible to traverse right ten feet to a ledge and set a good belay anchor. From here climb up and left until you are directly beneath a long, narrow roof with a crack on its right side. Turn this roof to a small ledge with a bolt. Next traverse right for six feet then climb up and left to the top of a large block which is at the right end of a long ledge. From here traverse left on the ledge to the point where one of the other routes intersects the ledge and follow Route 2 or Route 3 for the final pitch(es) to the top.

The Pulpit. Photo by David Benyak.

Several small pitons might be reassuring on the second pitch.

Route 5, Snake Eyes, II, 5.8. Three pitches, fair to good rock. The climb starts to the right of the steeply rising roof system on the south face, on a small belay stance 20 feet to the right. Begin up a short, clean crack and traverse right, around some short, steep walls, and up a brushy ramp system to a belay. The next pitch goes up a good 35-foot crack system to a belay below a steep wall. The third pitch traverses right to a steep corner with a small crack in the right side. Climb the crack (5.8) until you can traverse right on a sloping ramp and continue until it ends at a bolt. Climb 20 feet to a tree on the southeast ridge which is then followed to the top.

Lost Spectacle

Lost Spectacle is a small 200-foot pinnacle on the north side of upper La Cueva Canyon and about 200 yards up canyon from the Pulpit. It is separated from the main wall by a deep 70-foot notch. There are many variations up this formation with at least one on each side.

Route 1, Notch to West Face, I, 5.2. One pitch. This is a short, easy climb which begins at the base of the notch. Scramble up to the notch and then make your way around to the west side and then up to the top.

Route 2, Notch Direct, I, 5.5, A1. One pitch. Start at the very top of the notch and work up a shallow chimney for about 20 feet. Angle left from here to a face and free-climb to the top. Several aid placements are used in the lower and upper parts of the chimney.

Route 3, South Ridge, II, 5.7. Four or five pitches. Begin at the base of the south ridge just off La Luz Trail and continue up, staying on the ridge to the top. The climb is probably no harder than 5.4 or 5.5 except for one six-foot section.

Route 4, Mentally Vacuous Frippery, I, 5.10, A1. Two pitches. This route begins on the southwest face of Lost Spectacle. Climb diagonally up and right to a short dihedral which ends at a ledge beneath an overhang. The second pitch involves a short, very delicate traverse left on a clean face. Move up to a fixed aid piton (only one move of aid on the climb) which allows you to reach easier climbing up to a ledge. From here, move left to some large blocks. A short, easy section leads to the summit.

The climb was first done using all nuts except for the one fixed piton.

Route 5, Moonlight Serenade, II, 5.7, A2. Two pitches. Climbing is fairly sustained. This route is located on the south face of Lost Spectacle. Begin in a left-facing corner that forms the right-hand boundary of a large slab. Climb ten feet up the crack and move left and up slab to small ledges beneath steepening wall. Move six feet left and climb straight up over a slight bulge into a left-facing groove above. Continue up on aid as necessary to a ledge beneath an overhang. Climb left around roof and continue up to the second large ledge and set a belay. Begin the second pitch by freeclimbing up a right-hand corner to overhangs. Traverse 40 feet left on friction to fixed pitons then go around corner to left and up to the summit.

Yataghan

The Yataghan is a large, prominent buttress located on the north side of upper La Cueva Canyon east of the Pulpit. Access is by hiking up (or down) La Luz Trail. The standard descent from the top is a scramble back down to La Luz Trail via one of the brushy gullies which flanks the Yataghan.

Route 1, Southeast Face, III, 5.7. Difficulty of the climb is fairly sustained with good exposure. Quality of rock is fair. Six pitches. Start the climb in the narrow couloir between the Frog and the Yataghan at the broken red chimney 100 feet from the entrance to the couloir. Easy climbing leads up the chimney for 50 feet to a belay on the left. From here climb the chimney to its end and angle up and right to a belay on a broken ledge. The third pitch is long and goes up through a red gully adjacent to a flake, traverses left at its top and then to a small but prominent pine on a ledge. From here, two variations exist:

1. Exit the right side of the ledge and climb the indistinct corner above for 50 feet then traverse left past a bolt to a large ledge with pine trees, or

2. Exit left off the ledge and climb a crack in a right-facing corner to the large ledge above. This large ledge is called Lunch Ledge and is a good opportunity to do as its name suggests. The last two leads go straight up from the right end of Lunch Ledge.

The first variation is probably the easier, but in any case one ends up at Lunch Ledge. There is also a variation to the left from Lunch Ledge, which is judged to be somewhat harder than the standard route to the right. There are fixed pitons and/or bolts at several locations along the climb, depending upon the particular route chosen.

Route 2, East Face Variation, III, 5.7. This is a variation of the southeast face route. Begin at the base of the approach couloir, just left of a cave. Climb 150 feet to a large tree at the base of the second large step of the southeast ridge. Step around the corner of the ridge and angle right 200 feet up the east face, keeping below

Yataghan. Photo by David Benyak.

the overhangs. Join the first gully on the regular route and continue on.

Route 3, The Happy Gnome, III, 5.8. Six pitches. The crux lead is the fourth, with the other leads rated about 5.7. Quality of rock is fair. This climb is located on the west face of the Yataghan. Begin the climb up a brittle red dihedral roughly below the left side of a huge overhang which runs horizontally about three-fourths of the way up the face. The first lead follows this dihedral for about 130 feet to a platform on the left. Continue on for 40 feet, then traverse left about 30 feet in the middle of the second lead, then climb up a blank section such that the pitch ends in a hole at the bottom of the large dihedral. The third lead exits the hole to the left and ends with a partial hanging belay. The fourth and crux lead follows a nice crack up for 20 feet then traverses about 30 feet to the left on thin ledges and a small crack, ending under a large overhang just beneath a pine tree growing on its lip. Turn the overhang and set a hanging belay on the tree. The fifth lead follows straight up the crack above the tree ending on the large ledge mentioned in the Southeast Face description. The final lead follows the standard route (Southeast Face) to the summit.

Route 4, West Face Variation, III, 5.10. Six pitches. This route is a variation of Route 3. After the second pitch of Route 3, ascend the dihedral that goes up the left side of the face. Continue for two leads until 20 feet below the large overhangs. Then traverse right, joining pitch number 4 of the regular route, and proceed as in Route 3.

Route 5, Blood on the Blade, III, 5.10. Five pitches, good rock. Scramble up the gully between the Yataghan and the Frog and belay at the top of a fourth-class slab. Climb past a bolt and up 30 feet then back right to a fixed pin. Traverse 10 feet then climb up past a bolt to an overhang

(5.10) and belay above. The next pitch goes up a gully to a belay just left of a triangular face on a small ledge. Traverse left 10 feet to a crack on the Happy Gnome route then up to the top of a pedestal and a fixed-pin belay. Continue up and right past a bolt, mantle, and climb up to Lunch Ledge. Continue on the standard route to the summit.

Frog

This rib is located in upper La Cueva Canyon being just below the Yataghan to the southeast. A deep, brushy couloir with a huge chockstone at the entrance separates the Frog from the Yataghan. The Frog gets its name because of the prominent overhang below the summit which resembles a frog's head when viewed from the correct angle. Descend the Frog by walking off the back side and forcing an unpleasant bushwhack back down to La Luz Trail by way of the gully separating the Frog from Chaos Crag to the east.

Route 1, West Ridge, II, 5.7. Four pitches. Difficulty is mostly on the order of 5.5 to 5.6 with one or two 5.7 moves on the climb. Quality of rock is good except for some deterioration near the end of the climb. Start the climb at the base of the west ridge just to the right of the large chockstone blocking the entrance to the gully between the Frog and the Yataghan. Follow a clean crack up for 30 feet and then follow the line of least resistance, staying generally just to the right of the ridge. The first three leads are reasonably sustained with good rock and mostly good protection although one or two stretches are difficult to protect with nuts. Each of the first three leads has one or two fairly delicate moves. The final lead is a fourth-class scramble to the top over very loose rock. Beware of the large, loose flake directly above the belay ledge at the top of the first pitch.

Chaos Crag

This formation is the large rib above and to the east of the Frog. Approach by way of La Luz Trail.

Route 1, Southwest Face, III, 5.7(?) Four or five pitches. Climb 300 feet up the right sloping gully which starts to the left of midface up the couloir which separates Chaos Crag from the Frog. This gully leads to a wide ledge at midface just above a clump of fir trees. Climb two leads up a shallow gully to a V-shaped clump of trees just above a roofed crack located in the gully. Angle to the right to the summit notch and follow a crack system to the top.

Route 2, Metamorphosis, II, 5.7. Four pitches. The last two leads are the hardest with 5.7 climbing encountered on two short sections. These two leads are exposed but have good quality rock. Quality of rock is only fair on the first two leads. Begin just right of an ominous 40-foot dihedral which ends in a roof, just north of the south ridge of Chaos Crag. Pick your way up and right onto the south ridge and belay at a ledge. Climb the fourth-class gully above until it is possible to make a long traverse left to a fine grassy ledge on the west face which offers a spectacular view. This is Space Ledge. From Space Ledge follow the obvious right-facing dihedral at the north end of the ledge for 110 feet to a stance on the left. The fourth pitch either continues up this crack and through the rotten roof at its top or goes up for 10 feet then steps down and traverses right for 15 feet to an excellent crack which is followed to the top.

Route 2, Duck Soup, III, 5.9., A3 or 5.10. Four pitches. Begin at the base of the west face of Chaos Crag. Scramble up about 30 feet to a small pine tree just to the right of the center of the face. Climb disconnected cracks directly above for 130 feet to a belay on small ledges in a

The Frog with Yataghan in background. Photo by David Benyak.

corner. The second pitch goes up and right in the corner toward an ominous 20-foot red roof. Continue up, then step left to a bolt and continue left on partial aid to the base of a prominent crack system which angles left up the center of the face. Moderate climbing up this crack system leads another 30 feet to a belay ledge. Continue up the crack (which thins out at this point) on thin face holds or aid to a roof. Turn the roof (5.9) and run out the length of the rope to a belay in slings near the end of the crack. The final pitch goes up and slightly left to a bolt, then up on awkward aid through the roof. Eighty feet of moderate faceclimbing above leads to the summit.

El Paisano

This rock is on the way to Mexican Breakfast. From the notch above the Sentinel, drop down to the south and follow the left wall around for 100 yards.

Route 1, El Paisano, I, 5.9. One pitch. Locate the slab with a long, flat overhang. Climb an obvious crack up and through the roof. Traverse left and down to reach a ledge with a bolt and finish up and right. A few pitons are helpful.

Mexican Breakfast

This small formation is visible from La Luz Trail and is located immediately below Torreon. The easiest approach is to hike down from Sandia Crest to the base of the east side of the Sentinel. From here, drop down the south side of the ridge and follow the talus slopes down to the west side of Torreon. You should end up at the base of Torreon and immediately west of Mexican Breakfast.

Route 1, Mexican Breakfast Crack, I, 5.8 or 5.9. Two

Chaos Crag. Photo by David Benyak.

pitches. Sustained 5.8 crack climbing is encountered all the way up the first pitch with the crux occurring at the end of the first lead while escaping the large overhang. Quality of rock is excellent. The first lead is mostly an off-width jam crack with a hanging belay necessary at the end of the pitch. The second pitch may be done as either an off-width crack leading directly up from the overhang or as a slightly easier, but less protected, traverse to the right.

Route 2, Tarantula, I, 5.10. Two pitches. Excellent rock. Start on the thin crack in the face to the left of Mexican Breakfast Crack. Climb this crack to the roof then traverse left to an off-width crack at the left end of the overhang. Turn the overhang and continue left and up. One more easy pitch leads to the top of the formation.

Torreon

This huge buttress rises out of the upper part of La Cueva Canyon just behind Chaos Crag. The best approach is via the La Luz Trail. From the top, a rappel or downclimb to gain the notch is followed by a short scramble to Sandia Crest.

Route 1, Mountain Momma, III, 5.10. Seven pitches. Quality of rock is good. Start on the obvious shallow dihedral located on the south end of the west face and follow it up for two pitches. The first pitch ends at two bolts and the second pitch (5.10) ends on a good ledge beneath an intimidating corner. The third lead goes up and left for 25 feet past a bolt to a good ledge. From the ledge make some moves up on thin rock and continue bearing left to small ledges where an awkward belay is set. Above this belay is an obvious bulge with a crack running up it. Climb up and right, move past the bulge (5.10) and continue up the crack and over a roof (5.10).

Belay just above the roof. The next two pitches move up the face on 5.9 rock. Belay at the top of the sixth pitch in a chimney. The final lead is a short, easy pitch which brings you to a shoulder beneath the summit.

Route 2, Sorcerer's Apprentice, III, 5.10. Left of Mountain Momma is a large roof 300 feet above the ground with a clean 70-foot corner immediately to its left. Begin by following crack-flake systems which are beneath the right side of this roof. When these cracks end at a small roof, climb 40 feet higher and slightly left to a partially hanging stance. The second pitch goes up and around an awkward corner and past two bolts beneath a left-facing corner. Climb this corner to its end and belay beneath the clean 70-foot corner mentioned above. Climb this corner (5.10) and traverse 15 feet to a belay. Climb 160 feet up and right to a belay ledge above some bushes. Climb the corner above to the top.

Route 3, Wizard of Odd, III, 5.9+. Four pitches, good rock. Begin climbing at the toe of the south ridge of Torreon level with the top of the first pitch of Mountain Momma. Climb up 40 feet, then move left across a smooth face beneath a small roof to an airy stance at the very corner of the west face and south ridge. Climb left then up (5.9+) for 30 feet to a hanging belay. The second pitch goes up discontinuous cracks above the belay for 90 feet to the large prominent roof just left of the south ridge. Turn the roof on the left and climb a crack 50 feet to hanging belay near the end of the crack. The final two pitches gain the south ridge and follow it to broken ground below the summit.

Route 4, Bitch's Brew, III, 5.11. Five pitches. Climb the first two pitches of Mountain Momma but instead of belaying at the ledge at the end of the second pitch, continue up the crack to the right, past a bolt (5.10) to a belay 10 feet higher up. From here, perform a desperate

Torreon with Mexican Breakfast in the lower left foreground. Photo by David Benyak.

layback up an overhanging crack and continue on easier crack climbing to a roof above. Faceclimb right to a good ledge and up the overhanging wall above. One more pitch above the wall leads to the top.

Rat's Rock

Rat's Rock is the formation located just southeast of Torreon. "Descend" from the summit of Rat's Rock by hiking up to the crest.

Route 1, Lost Hole, II, 5.7. Five pitches. Quality of rock is poor to good. From La Luz Trail near Donald Duck, Lost Hole can be recognized by a wide, slightly left-leaning crack situated directly below the overhangs near the summit. From the base of the rock the crack can just be seen just below a hole in the summit overhangs.

Begin by scrambling up a short, right-facing dihedral and set a belay from a tree. Climb the dihedral and scramble 40 feet to fourth-class rock. Climb ten feet to a ledge and belay. The next lead goes up a jigsaw crack on the left side of the ledge, then traverses right and up beneath an overhang to a wide, left-facing dihedral and belay. The third lead goes straight up to overhanging rock then up broken blocks on the left to a belay just below a wide, left-leaning crack. The next lead continues to the base of the crack then up the crack (5.7), exiting over loose blocks. Climb up broken rock to a belay, 20 feet below a hole created by a large chockstone suspended between overhangs. Finish the climb by climbing 40 feet through the hole to the summit.

Route 2, Bombs Away, II, 5.9. Three pitches, good rock. This climb ascends the roofs just left of Lost Hole. Start by scrambling up to a small tree on a blocky ledge above and left of the start to the Lost Hole route. Climb up easy faces and belay on a blocky ledge. Climb left off the ledge through a section of loose-looking, but usually solid, rock and continue up good rock toward the roofs above, traversing left under the roof. Climb the roof and belay a few feet higher on a ledge. The last pitch finishes up easy rock, through the Lost Hole to the top. Small wired nuts are useful on this climb.

Route 3, Behind Blue Eyes, II, 5.8. Three pitches, rock is good. This route ascends the northwestern portion of Rat's Rock up the prominent chimney on the upper part of the face. Start by following the first pitch of Bombs Away. The second pitch traverses left all the way to the end of the ledge and onto the face and up to the end of a bush-covered ramp to belay. The next pitch (crux) goes up a crack, through a bush, and left to the base of the prominent chimney. Climb the chimney and exit through a squeeze hole at a group of chockstones at the top.

Fin

The Fin is the obvious rib which sits just north of La Luz Trail and just up the trail from Donald Duck. It is situated in a north-south direction with its ridgeline running roughly perpendicular to the trail.

Route 1, Exhibition Wall, A1/A2(?) or 5.10. Two pitches. Begin at the lower north side of the red portion of the overhanging east face. The first lead goes up a diagonal crack to the left and then underneath a large chockstone which is loosely situated on the wall. Traverse 15 feet left on a ledge above the chockstone and climb up to a smaller ledge at which a belay bolt is placed. The second lead proceeds straight up and then escapes to the right of a roof, ending beside a pine tree on the summit. Traverse south along the summit ridge to gain the trail.

The first pitch was climbed without aid (5.10) on a subsequent ascent.

Route 2, North Ridge, I, 5.8. One pitch. Begin in the obvious dihedral at the base of the north ridge. Climb through a broken area above the dihedral and turn the prominent roof directly via the crack (a number 11 hexcentric comes in handy). Traverse right above the roof and climb easy rock to a two-bolt belay ledge near the large dead tree visible on the ridge. From this point, fourth class the rest of the way to the top and down the other side.

Donald Duck

This structure sits just off La Luz Trail to the south in upper La Cueva Canyon. It gets its name from the unusual formation on the summit that resembles its namesake when viewed from the east on La Luz Trail.

Route 1, Northeast Corner, I, 5.6. One pitch. Quality of rock is fair to good. Start the climb in the red open book approximately on the northeast corner. Near the top of the wide crack traverse to the right to attain the summit. This climb can also be top roped as the summit is accessible by scrambling up from the back side.

Fire Hydrant

This stubby pinnacle lies north and west of Donald Duck and is situated lower down and closer to the trail. The two formations are separated by a deep couloir.

Route 1, Northwest Face, I, 5.6. One pitch. Start at the notch on the north side of the Fire Hydrant and proceed up the northwest face. Follow a crack up and traverse to the north face and continue up to some ledges. Traverse left from the ledges across a chimney and proceed along the ridges to the top. Rappel off a bolt down the southeast side of Fire Hydrant opposite Donald Duck.

Paired Pole Pillars

This is a twin-summitted formation which is located just south of La Luz Trail and southeast of the Fin. There is a west and east summit, each of which has a pole affixed on top. Reach the Paired Pole Pillars by climbing down via La Luz Trail. Routes 1 and 2 climb the westernmost pillar while Routes 3 and 4 lead up the eastern pillar.

Route 1, North Gully, I, A1(?). One pitch. Begin up a deceptive stone-filled crack covered with rock lettuce. Thirty feet up, traverse left and climb to the top of the gully. Climb around a corner and traverse across the lower northwest face, continuing to the summit via Route 2.

Route 2, Northwest Face, I, 5.6. One pitch. Quality of rock is good. Begin climb on west face, traversing over the corner to the northwest face after about 25 feet up. Continue on up an open book and then on up the northwest face for the remainder of the climb, angling right to the summit. Protection is poor to fair for the bottom part of the climb. A fixed piton protects the crux move on the northwest face.

Route 3, Southeast Corner, I, 5.4(?). One pitch. This short climb begins at the notch on the southeast side. Follow an obvious crack perhaps 50 feet in length to the summit.

Route 4, Northeast Corner, I, 5.6. Start from the lowest point on the east face. Angle right to a steep face on the northeast corner. Climb up this face and traverse on thin ledges to the east face and finish direct to the top.

Route 5, Plimsolls, I, 5.8. Two pitches. Rock is good. Start on the north buttress of the pillar closest to the trail and climb a wide, shallow chimney with cracks at the back to a large blocky belay ledge. Climb up some blocks and step onto the west side for 60 feet of sustained climbing followed by a traverse left, above a small roof. Continue up a crack system then traverse left to a corner and up to a brushy ledge. Finish straight up and walk off to the south.

Estrellita

This is a small rock formation in upper La Cueva Canyon. Approach by hiking down the La Luz Trail from the crest. Continue down the trail until you are at the base of Redeemer on a north switchback in the trail. From here continue down the trail to the base of the Paired Pole Pillars at a south switchback. From this switchback walk north to the next switchback which should have a flat spot and continue north off the trail for about 50 yards until you come to Estrellita.

Route 1, I, 5.8. One pitch. The climb starts in a very prominent crack that is in a small corner. After 15 feet the crack turns a small roof and subsequently becomes a straight-in jam which is followed to a dihedral. Follow the dihedral for about half its distance then step out to the left and follow a crack 30 feet more up a very steep face. Traverse left to a belay stance on a broken ledge near the summit. Cross the ledge and descend via a third-class gully.

Redeemer

The Redeemer is one of the uppermost granite formations in La Cueva Canyon. Its summit appears to be a small pinnacle situated just below the first switchback below the intersection of La Luz and Crest Spur trails. Reach the base of this wall by hiking down the trail (five switchbacks) below this intersection. Descend from the summit by scrambling directly across the backside to the La Luz Trail.

Route 1, I, 5.5. Two pitches. Contour north of the trail around a good-sized rock outcropping to the base of a large couloir. The west wall of the couloir has a right-sloping crack system which provides the main portion of the climb. Begin climbing up a sharply angled dihedral and continue up along the crack system to a good belay ledge. The second lead continues angling to the right and then goes left up a gully to a large, balanced flake. From this flake, traverse right and finish up a series of friction slabs.

Route 2, Occasional Freshman, II, 5.7. Three pitches. Located on the west face of Redeemer, this route is fairly sustained in difficulty. Begin the first lead 20 feet up and right of the bottom of the face in a left-facing dihedral. Work up then right out of the dihedral and up the face to a ledge. The second lead climbs up from the ledge keeping to the crack slightly to the left (do not take the groove on the right) and up the loose blocks which form a chimney. Exit left onto a ledge and continue up right until you are behind the huge flake. Bridge up onto the large chockstone then move into a squeeze chimney and work up to the top of the flake. The final lead begins with a hand traverse eight feet to the left (5.7+) and then leads straight up to the ridge and then to the summit.

Route 3, Northwest Corner, II, 5.8. Two pitches. This route is fairly sustained in difficulty. Begin the climb 30 feet up and left from the bottom of the face. Climb a short wall (15 feet) onto a ledge. Go right around the corner and climb the leftmost chimney (with bush) to a steep slab. Traverse several feet left and then straight up past the bush to an awkward alcove. Continue up the obvious crack to a ledge. The second lead follows a crack in the wall above until you reach sloping platforms, then follow the ridge up to the summit.

Hole in the Wall

This formation is a west-facing slab just north of the Redeemer. At the base of the rock is the old La Luz Mine. Approach by hiking north at the fifth switchback down on the La Luz Trail and hike past the Redeemer, keeping to the base of the rock, until you come to the mine entrance. Exit the top of the face by bushwhacking up to the La Luz Trail.

Route 1, Miss Piggy, I, 5.8. Two pitches, good rock, sustained climbing. Begin at the base of the detached flake up and to the left of the mine entrance. Climb the center of the flake and up to the crack which breaches the smooth face extending across the lower part of the buttress. Above the crack (5.8), turn the corner to the right and cross easy rock to the pine tree on the large belay ledge at the center of the face. The next pitch goes to the left and up a crack system (5.7+) and continues straight up the face. Exit over a large chockstone at the top.

Thumb

The Thumb is the prominent formation that dominates the south side of upper La Cueva Canyon. Its blade-like shape makes the Thumb appear as a sharp pinnacle when viewed edgewise from the northwest. When viewed from the east or west, the Thumb can be identified by its broad faces capped by twin summits. The standard approach is via La Luz Trail from the

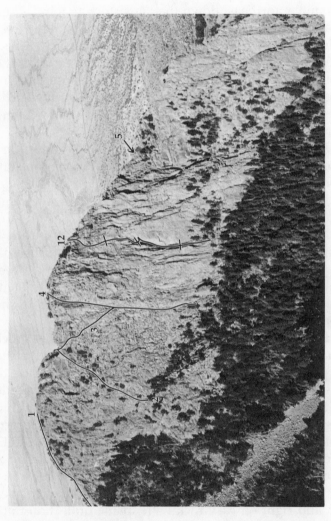

East face of the Thumb. Photo by David Benyak.

crest. The standard route of descent is to downclimb the southeast ridge from the south summit and then scramble northeast down the talus slope to join La Luz Trail. The routes on the southwest face start on the tree-studded slopes at the lower part of the face. These slopes can be reached from the notch at the base of the southeast ridge (which involves some exposed down-climbing or a rappel) or from the northwest ridge. The west side of the Thumb can also be reached by hiking directly up La Cueva Canyon.

Route 1, Southeast Ridge, 3. Although rated third class the nonclimber would probably find the exposure un-comfortable. Reach the climb by scrambling up the talus slope to the notch just below the ridge, follow the ridge up keeping to the left.

Route 2, East Face, 5.8. Four pitches. Quality of rock is fair to good. The climb starts on the east face just south of and below the summit notch. Angle right up tree-covered ledges then finish direct to the summit notch. A short fourth-class pitch leads from the notch to the south summit.

Route 3, East Face Direct, II, 5.8. Four pitches, rock quality variable. This climb begins at the base of the large crack which runs directly up the east face to the north summit. Climb up a crack on the right side of the open book and at the highest point move right to a small platform and continue up and left to a comfort-able belay. From here, traverse left (5.8) then up until the dihedral pinches off, and eventually up to a belay at the major crack system. Climb up on loose rock and through a chimney to the next belay. The last pitch goes up and right on easy rock with sparse protection until you reach the ridge.

Route 4, North Summit Direct, II, 5.7 or 5.8. Four pitches? Begin as in Route 3. Instead of angling left out

West face of the Thumb. Photo by David Benyak.

of the large crack at the end of one pitch, continue up the main crack to the north summit.

Route 5, Northwest Ridge, III, 5.5. Eight to 15 pitches. Quality of rock is good. The most difficult portion of the climb is concentrated in the first four leads. The remainder of the climb is third- or fourth-class with the possible exception of the last lead. To reach the start of the climb, hike down La Luz Trail near the bottom of the talus slope to the first switchback above the point where the stream crosses the trail and travel horizontally west, scrambling up to an obvious ledge on the ridge which has a small tree on it. The climb can also be started some 150 feet farther down at the base of the ridge. The route for the first several pitches stays to the left of the ridge. Climbing the ridge direct results in a more difficult climb.

This is probably the most frequently climbed fifth-class route on the Thumb. It has good exposure and a spectacular view. Allow a full day for the climb.

Route 6, Southwest Chimney, III, 5.5 or 5.6. From the bottom of the wide ledges leading from the northwest ridge climb up the outcropping which is made up of a series of ledges. From a large grassy ramp at the top of this outcropping, climb a friction slab and then go up the face to a couple of fir trees. From the trees, climb over some large ledges up to a layback which ends at the base of the chimney. The chimney is quite wide and difficult but opens out onto a short walk to the summit notch.

Route 7, III, 5.5 or 5.6. This climb starts on the huge tree-covered ramp which diagonals up the west side of the Thumb. Begin below and to the left of the summit notch and climb up the right side of the obvious outcropping. From the grassy ramp at the top of the outcropping the route coincides with Route 6 as far as the two fir trees. Complete the climb by traversing left at this point on a series of broken ledges to the northwest ridge and follow it to the summit. *Route 8*, III, 5.6. Six pitches. Difficulty is intermittent and sustained only on the last lead. Quality of rock is good. Begin halfway up the tree-covered ramp which begins below the summit notch on the west face, just to the right of the black waterstreaks. The climb angles up to the right and follows a line which leads up steeper rock and curves back to the left, intersecting the southeast ridge shortly below the summit.

Route 9, Waterstains Route, II, 5.8. Four pitches. This climb goes up the black water streaks which are located below the notch between the double summits on the west face of the Thumb. Quality of rock is mostly good but the nature of the rock is such that it may be difficult to place protection using nuts. Reach the climb by cutting across the present La Luz Trail or by hiking up La Cueva Canyon and, in either case, by scrambling around the base of the northwest ridge to the base of the obvious waterstains. Climb up the waterstains. The first lead involves face climbing (5.7) followed by easier climbing with the next belay 100 feet up. The second pitch goes up a broken, left-facing dihedral with a 5.8 crux move. The third pitch goes up to a 5.7 face. Traverse right then up, ending at a position below the notch. Finish the climb with a fourth-class scramble to the south summit.

Route 10, Muralla Blanca, III, 5.9. Five pitches. Quality of rock is excellent. Climb begins from a large ramp below the southwest face which is reached by scrambling down from the notch at the base of the southwest ridge. There is 5.8 free climbing on a short dihedral section of the second lead and immediately following the hard moves on the fourth lead. This climb is sometimes done with the first pitch omitted as it is possible to third class horizontally to the start of the second pitch.

Route 11, Zonker's Folly, III, 5.8. Five pitches. Quality of rock is good. The first two leads are the same as for Muralla Blanca. The crux is on the second lead and consists of a short dihedral (5.8) followed by a 5.7 off-width crack above a dead tree. A 5.7 mantle on the third lead can be avoided by climbing to the left but the protection is poor. After the fourth lead, scramble up a wide chimney to the base of the final lead, but watch for loose rock in the chimney. Finish just below the south summit on the southeast ridge.

Route 12, Aviary Ort Overhangs, III, 5.9. Four pitches. Difficulty is rather sustained with each of the first three leads rating 5.8 or harder. Quality of rock is mostly fair to good but becomes loose above the overhanging dihedral.

Begin the climb at the bottom of the prominent overhanging dihedral on the east face and climb 130 feet to a hanging belay beneath a roof. Turn the roof (5.8) then continue on up the crack, turn another overhang after about 60 feet, and traverse up onto the face 40 feet to the right ending on a small belay ledge in a slight hollow. On the third lead traverse back into the dihedral to the left, climb a flake, then move up and right (5.9) beneath a roof, exiting its right side. Climb through the top of the dihedral above and up about 30 feet more through large, loose blocks. Set a belay just below a steep crack which forms the start of the large rock lettuce-covered open book which the fourth pitch follows to the ridge just north of the north summit. Watch for loose rock on the final pitch.

Tridents

The Tridents are located just east of the Thumb and

are approached by scrambling up the large talus slopes between the Tridents and the Thumb. The climbs listed below are all located on the broad west face of the fin-like formation which faces the Thumb. The Tridents themselves are the three small, not particularly obvious, pinnacles which sit atop the formation. The descent route from the Tridents involves scrambling down the north side to the talus slopes above La Luz Trail.

Route 1, Potwana, I, 5.7. Three pitches. Quality of rock is good. The first lead is the crux. Begin the climb at the center of a shallow buttress which is located roughly in the middle of the west face. Climb up a small, clean crack to an aspen-covered ramp. From the ramp, angle up and left below an overhang. Traverse left under the overhang and mantle up out a grassy ledge (5.7). From the grassy ledge perform the most unique and committing move of the climb. This involves a leap in order to grab an obvious rock point in the shape of a ship's prow off to the right. If you make this move (5.6) successfully, mantle up to a large ledge and belay from a pair of trees. The second pitch follows a distinct dihedral and then traverses right past trees on a small ledge. Belay from a large rubble-covered ledge. The final pitch angles to the right and reaches the summit after intermittent scrambling.

Route 2, Lost Line, II, 5.6. Five pitches. Quality of rock is fair. This climb starts in a chimney at the base of the prominent crack closest to the trail on the west face just above Donald Duck. Begin up the chimney and traverse to the right at the first opportunity, following a buttress on up to the base of a wall. Belay from a large boulder on an obvious ledge. The second pitch follows a series of cracks to a belay stance on the ridgeline. The third lead goes over a prominent gendarme and belays from a tree. The fourth lead goes up a forked crack on a smooth face and ends at a large boulder. The last pitch involves a short ramp followed by scrambling the rest of the way to the top.

Route 3, 5.10 Squirrel, II, 5.6. Five pitches. Quality of rock is fair. Start the climb at the base of the second obvious crack up from La Luz Trail on the west face. Set the first belay after scrambling up to a group of trees on a dirt-covered ledge. The first lead goes up and left over broken slabs. Slip behind a large flake and chimney up until it is possible to escape to the left around a corner, and on to a long ledge. Traverse the length of the ledge and belay from a tree. A horizontal piton may be needed to protect the last few moves of this pitch. The second pitch follows any one of several, mostly easy, lines up to the ridge. The last three pitches are the same as for Lost Line.

Route 4, Narrow Escape, III, 5.8. Six pitches, good rock. This climb starts up the north ridge of the Tridents which you reach by scrambling up from the La Luz Trail and up several ledges to the base. Climb up to an obvious yellow roof with a fixed pin, then traverse right on a ramp to the corner and continue up the corner until you can traverse back to a belay stance next to a large yellow wall. The next pitch starts up a short groove (5.7+ or 5.8) between the belayer and the yellow wall and works back to the corner on the right. The direct variation goes directly up the ridge on a 5.8 crack system; the Narrow Escape variation avoids this by going out across a face to the right on a thin balance ledge and ends at a belay in trees at the other side of the face. The next three or four pitches more or less follow the ridge on up to the summit.

Route 5, Misty Ridge, I, 5.6. Three pitches, fair rock. This climb goes up the east ridge of the Tridents. Approach by scrambling up scree slopes to the east side of the Tridents to the base of a wide crack interrupted by a bush-covered ledge. The first pitch goes up this crack to a good belay ledge. From here, climb the formation to the right then cross over and work down to a belay stance between the east ridge and the true summit. One final easy pitch leads to the summit.

Route 6, Debaucher's Deluxe, II, 5.7. Four pitches, fair rock. This climb goes up the south ridge of the Tridents. Make your way to the notch between the east side of the Tridents and the Point and continue to the south, past a rib of rock, to the base of the south ridge next to a nice spire. Climb up the corner of the ridge next to the spire, bearing left, on 5.7 rock and belay beneath a small roof next to a chimney. Climb the chimney (5.7) until you can exit to the left and continue up on easy rock to a belay on good ledges. The third pitch (5.6) goes up and right, following a nice dihedral and ends at a tree on the left at the top of the dihedral. Third- and fourth-class climbing leads the rest of the way to the summit.

Upper Domingo Baca Canyon and Vicinity

The Upper Domingo Baca Canyon area was the last significant climbing area in the Sandias to attract climbing activity. Many fine rock formations exist here including Hail Peak, Jawbone, Ego Boost, Pino Wall, Alioth, and others. This rugged section can be seen firsthand by the tram rider on the upper half of his ride to the upper tram terminal.

Climbs in Upper Domingo Baca can be reached by hiking up the canyon but it is more common to approach from the top. The most straightforward way to approach many of the climbs is via Echo Canyon, but the uninitiated must be warned that there is no easy way to approach climbs in Domingo Baca Canyon. To reach Echo Canyon, hike down the La Luz Trail from either the crest or the Summit House to the junction where the two forks of the trail join. Immediately south of this junction is a gully that represents the upper extremity of Echo Canyon. One can either hike down this gully or the next one to the south, and in either case, difficult bushwhacking leads down Echo Canyon to its entrance which is framed by Hail Peak to the east and Ego Boost to the west. A somewhat easier approach to Hail Peak can be made by hiking south on the La Luz Trail from the junction to a point where the trail makes a sharp bend to the north and east (below Kiwanis Cabin). At this point there is a vista overlook, referred to as Domingo Baca overlook, marked by a sign, which can be hiked down from to reach Hail Peak. This latter approach is difficult enough in its description that I won't attempt it here. One other approach to the upper Domingo Baca Canyon area is via TWA Canyon. This canyon was named after a TWA Super Constellation that crashed in the canyon in the 1950s. The canyon is located on the other side of Hail Peak from Echo Canyon. The head of the canyon is located below the La Luz Trail east of the overlook below Kiwanis Cabin but before the trail curves back to the south.

The final approach route is to hike up Domingo Baca Canyon from the bottom.

The Point

The Point is the prominent formation with a smooth-looking ramp south of a large gully at the extreme north end of the west wall of Echo Canyon. Its ultimate summit forms the apex of the ridge that leads southwest from the junction where the La Luz Trail splits. Approach the climbs by descending Echo Canyon from the La Luz Trail fork.

Route 1, Power of Words, II, 5.8. Two or three pitches. Rock is good. This climb goes up the right side of a large alcove that has two small caves to the left. Scramble up the apron in the alcove to a grass ledge below a group of red roofs. The route ascends the dihedral to the right. The first pitch climbs a steep crack in the face of the dihedral to a small belay stance. The second pitch goes left into the open book and up to a belay on small wired nuts. A final short pitch gains the summit ridge.

Route 2, Sid Vicious, II, 5.10. Three pitches. Rock is good. Scramble up the ramp of the Point and begin the climb where the gully to the north is joined. Climb up about 60 feet to a bolt on the ramp face and proceed to the middle of the ramp past a small ledge and into a dirt-filled crack. At the top of this crack traverse left on a ledge and belay by a bush. The next pitch involves sustained 5.9 and 5.10 climbing up the corner of the ramp and the left wall. Belay just beyond where the ramp pinches out. The remainder of the climb makes its way over easier rock to the top.

Yucca Flower Tower

This is a smooth buttress that is located on the east wall of Echo Canyon across from the Point. It leans back near the top and is split by three crack systems.

Route 1, III, 5.7, A3. Three to four pitches. The route lies in the rightmost crack of Yucca Flower Tower. Scramble up third class below the face to a blocky belay ledge near a large tree. Climb on awkward aid through the overhangs near the right edge of the face. Above the overhangs, thin nailing leads to a long, clean crack descending from the headwall above. Climb this crack with aid over the headwall, then climb free up broken rock to where the main crackline begins again. Aid up another headwall and exit right with freeclimbing near the top. At this point the face becomes slabby, and an easy pitch leads up to a notch. The final pitch climbs the steep headwall above via a clean jamcrack, then a delicate traverse left to an easier dihedral. From there, fourth-class leads to the rim. About fifty feet uphill from the rim is the La Luz Trail. Knifeblades are handy.

La Vista

La Vista is a large buttress northeast of Hail Peak on the east side of Echo Canyon. The upper section has two noticeable dihedrals, one facing left and one facing right with a series of red roofs in it. Approach from the Domingo Baca overlook below the La Luz Trail and hike down the gully toward Hail Peak. Keep to the right, past Hail Peak, traversing below two small spires and into a gully that runs in front of La Vista. Continue up this until you reach another gully coming off La Vista. Follow this up a short distance to the right end of a wide, smooth, steep face with two horizontal breaks in it.

Route 1, La Vista, III, 5.8. Six pitches. Rock and protection are good. Begin the climb below a large block about 30 feet up and set the belay for the first pitch just left of the block. The next three pitches wander up the face, aiming for a large, left-facing dihedral. From the left end of the belay ledge at the top of the third pitch, climb up this sustained dihedral and traverse left out of the dihedral 10 feet below a white pillar, and through a small overhang to a small belay stance. The fifth pitch goes straight up until a traverse left can be made and then up to a cluster of roofs (belay if windy). Traverse left and up a short arete to the left of the largest overhang of the cluster. Another 50 feet of climbing leads to a belay with the remainder of the climb being third class. Thin pitons may be helpful on this climb.

Route 2, Against the Wind, III, 5.10. Seven pitches. Rock and protection are good. Follow La Vista route as it is described above (Route 1) ending the fourth pitch in a hanging belay at the white pillar. The fifth pitch goes straight up from the pillar for 35 feet and ends at a belay at a small stance. The sixth pitch traverses right, goes up, then back left to a crack which involves sustained climbing up to a belay. Another short pitch ends in a third-class gully.

Other Echo Canyon Routes

Bush Shark Spire, I, 5.9. Two pitches. Rock and protection are good. Bush Shark Spire is situated on the east side of Echo Canyon and sticks out from the main face. Approach from the top of Echo Canyon or rappel the east side. The first pitch goes up a hand crack on the west face of the spire and ends on a nice but small ledge. The second pitch goes a short distance up, then left, and then back up and right to the original crack system which leads to the summit. A variation goes to the col between the summit and the canyon wall. Descend via a rappel off fixed pins at the notch or continue up Garden Party.

Garden Party, II, 5.9. Four or five pitches when combined with Bush Shark Spire. Rock and protection are good. Climb Bush Shark Spire and from the col behind the spire traverse right past a wide chimney system to a bushy ledge. From here drop down a little and hand traverse under a bulge in the wall to a short dihedral then up to a belay next to a crack system with a chimney at the top. The next pitch traverses into the crack system and up into the chimney where easier climbing leads to the top of the chimney. A short lead finishes the climb. This climb, exclusive of Bush Shark Spire, would be rated 5.8+.

Westeron Wynde, III, 5.9. Three or four pitches. Good rock and protection. This climb is located on the east side of Echo Canyon, just south of Bush Shark Spire. From the spire, follow the wall around and up into a large gully. Scramble up to large pines below a large crack system. The first pitch goes up the crack (5.9) and then traverses left into another crack system which is followed to a belay below a small roof. The second pitch turns the roof up the crack until it steepens and pinches out. Traverse left and up the face to a belay at a small fir tree. The third pitch goes up three consecutive mantel shelves (5.8 or 5.9) and then right, into a corner with a crack that is followed up to a bulge (5.9) with a belay 25 feet farther up. Another short, easy pitch finishes the climb.

Fear of Flying, III, 5.8, A4. Good rock. This climb goes up the south face of Techweeny Buttress, the obvious flat-topped rock at the head of Echo Canyon. Approach is down a gully between Techweeny Buttress and the Point. The climb starts at the junction of the south and west face. Traverse right past a bolt to gain access to the crack system. Follow the crack around the corner and up to a hanging belay. A 5.6 pitch up a wide crack leads to the top.

Increasingly Dred, I, 5.10. Three pitches. Approach by walking down and north from Domingo Baca overlook and descend the second gully from the overlook to the bottom of Echo Canyon. The climb is immediately to your left. The first pitch goes to the top of a pillar which leans against the main wall. The next pitch goes up the corner above the pillar, then left to steep face climbing with big ledges. Pass the small overhang (5.8) and belay on the large ledge above. The last pitch (5.10) climbs the dihedral, an off-width through the roof, and steep rock above ending atop a small pinnacle which is descended on the other side into the approach gully. An escape into the approach gully may also be made at the top of the second pitch.

Ego Boost

Ego Boost is a major rib which lies roughly north-south and is located east of the second tram tower, and west across Echo Canyon from Hail Peak. Its name results from the audience produced by nearby tram riders. Approach Ego Boost by scrambling up Domingo Baca Canyon or by hiking down to the fork in the La Luz Trail and scrambling down Echo Canyon. The descent route off Ego Boost is located on the west side. Start by downclimbing a small north-facing dihedral then traversing north on a sloping tree-studded ledge until you can see a wide gully below. Make one 75-foot rappel to the gully. The final 15 feet can either be downclimbed or a short rappel can be made.

Route 1, Southeast Ridge, I, 5.7. Two pitches with an additional 200 feet of third class. Quality of rock is good. Begin by scrambling 100 feet up to the top of the rock bench at the base of the southeast ridge. The first lead is short and relatively easy, leading over some large blocks to the right. The second pitch traverses diagonally up and left to the south face amphitheatre. Mantle onto a small grassy ledge to the right then layback onto an undercut slab (hard 5.7) and crack climb a few feet to a large flake. Finger traverse beneath a bulge across the top of the slab to a chockstone wedged in the bulge above a thorny bush, pull up and over the chockstone and belay. Tricky third-class rock leads to the summit ridge.

Route 2, Hang Glide, II, 5.8. Three pitches with an additional 200 feet of easy third class. Excellent rock. The climb begins up the wide, prominent crack which goes up the center of the southwest face. This prominent crack terminates at an overhang on the second pitch. The crux is climbing out of the crack to the left below the overhang.

Route 3, Diagonal, III, 5.9. Five to seven pitches plus 150 feet of third class. Quality of rock varies from poor to excellent. Difficulty on this climb is moderately sustained. Start the climb from a belay on top of a small, flat boulder situated in the upper east corner of the south face amphitheatre. Traverse left from the boulder on loose and unprotectable rock for 30 feet to the center of the amphitheatre above overhanging rock. Climb 15 feet to a nice horizontal crack and belay. Begin the second pitch by traversing a few feet to the right and climbing a short crack to a ledge covered with loose blocks. On the left side of the ledge is a dihedral with a bulge near its base (5.8). A small ledge above the bulge can be used for a belay or the lead can be extended 40 feet to the next belay. Continue up the dihedral to an enormous overhang and exit left onto a ledge with a huge flake on it and belay from the flake. Above the flake is a long crack that runs diagonally up and to the right for about 200 feet all the way to the southeast ridge. The next two leads follow this diagonal crack. The crux of this section occurs on the sixth pitch when you climb a section of wavy rock to a very small ledge then climb down and around a small corner and hand traverse (5.8) the final few feet of the diagonal crack. Belay from the southeast ridge. The final fifth-class pitch involves an easy mantle below an undercut slab then a layback over the undercut (hard 5.7) after which you follow a widening crack to a large block. Finger traverse right to a thorn bush with a chockstone above it. Pull over the chockstone and belay. A final section of tricky third class leads to the summit ridge.

Alioth

Alioth is a double-summitted formation bounded by Echo Canyon to the west and TWA Canyon to the east. It is located just northeast of Hail Peak. To reach Alioth, hike down La Luz Trail from the crest and go south on the branch that leads to the Summit House. Walk past the Domingo Baca overlook to where the trail curves north then back east. Drop down into TWA Canyon at this point following game trails on the left side. Continue past a large wall on the right (Block Ridge). A narrow canyon separates Block Ridge from Alioth which is next on the right.

Return from the climb by way of the broken ridge which connects Alioth with the main ridgeline below La Luz Trail.

Route 1, Alioth's Nose, III, 5.8, A2. Six pitches to the lower summit. The nose is south facing and 80 feet right of the 100-foot flake on Alioth's southwest face. The first pitch starts up a small rib 30 feet to the left of the nose. Ascend the rib and move up and right (5.7) to a decomposed gully on the nose. Climb to a roomy ledge system 175 feet up on the right. The third pitch moves up to the left of a small overhang (5.8), then 60 feet up and right, then traverses left around the ridge to a decomposed gully (a variation ascends a crack system up and left after passing the overhang). The next lead becomes increasingly difficult as the rock steepens. Ascend a crack heading toward the obvious break in the overhang.

Move left (5.8) out of the crack and onto the face, then up to a small belay stance below the overhang. The crux pitch goes A2 for ten feet through the overhang, and two rope lengths of freeclimbing up and left lead to the lower summit.

Route 2, East Ridge, II, 5.6. Three or four pitches. The east ridge is formed by the large east face and the couloir forming the back side of Alioth. Just left of the actual ridge on the lower east wall is a series of broken ledges. Ascend these ledges and then straight up dark, weathered cracks to a series of ledges which lead right to the ridge. Two leads over easy ledges follow the ridge to the summit.

Route 3, West Chimney, II, 5.6. The West Chimney is the obvious chimney on the southwest side which ascends directly to the lower summit. Fourth class to the notch between the summits and ascend the southwest face to the summit. Downclimb or rappel north from the lower summit down to the notch.

Route 4, Block Ridge Edge, II, 5.7. Block Ridge outlines the large face which is on your right while descending TWA Canyon just northeast of Alioth. A large block can be seen on top of the ridge.

Third class the ridge until forced to rope up. Climb up slightly to the right (5.7) for two devious pitches over decomposed rock. Traverse up and left from the base of a large crack to a roomy, sloping ledge. Climb the dihedral at the back corner to where it steepens then traverse left and up onto the broken ridgeline. Fourth class the top of the ridge.

Route 5, Last Goodbye, III, 5.8. Five pitches. Rock and protection good. This climb ascends the south ridge of Block Ridge. Locate the arete-like formation northeast of Alioth. Approach by bushwhacking down TWA Canyon and upon the shoulder of the ridge about 200 feet above the actual base of the ridge. Belay at a small pine tree. The first pitch goes up through a short overhanging groove (5.7) and up steep rock past a fixed pin. Traverse left into the obvious corner and up (5.8) to a belay at the top. The second pitch goes right and up for 25 feet then back left to a ridge and then wanders up to a belay by huge blocks. The third pitch goes a little right and up to a steep face. Go round the corner to the left and on top of the ridge. The fourth pitch runs the rope out along the ridge to the base of the large square block that can be seen from the trail. The final pitch goes up the steep face behind the block. A #10 hex and thin pitons are helpful.

Hail Peak

Hail Peak is the large twin-summitted formation which is situated in upper Domingo Baca Canyon. It also forms the lower east wall of Echo Canyon and is separated by a deep notch from the crest wall to the north. Reach Hail Peak by descending down Echo Canyon or by the approach down TWA Canyon. The descent from the south end of Hail Peak can be accomplished as follows: from the southern summit ridge hike 20 yards to a gully on the west side. Make a 75-foot rappel to the gully below. Follow the gully down until it becomes necessary to rappel again. A 110-foot rappel ends at a large ledge. From the large ledge downclimb in a northerly direction aiming for the top of the ridge that divides the west face of Hail Peak. Climb down this tree-covered ridge, called the "Bowling Alley," to the ground. If using only one rope, it is necessary to break the second rappel up into sections with both climbers hanging from slings at the end of the first rappel.

From the north end of the peak descend by downclimbing to the upper portion of the large ramp on the north side. Scramble down the ramp to the ground below.

Route 1, North Ramp, I, 5.3. Three pitches (?). Scramble up a gully starting on the northeast corner and rising toward the west. The gully opens into the broad rock ramp. At the top of the ramp climb a broken dihedral or make a traverse up to the left across the headwall to a notch just northwest of the summit. Quality of rock is good. The approach to the climb is a miserable bushwhack down a gully from La Luz Trail.

Route 2, Windy Ridge, III, 5.7. Six or seven pitches. First pitch is 5.7, the remaining leads are 5.4 to 5.6. This route is located on the south ridge of Hail Peak. It begins either at the base of the ridge or in a large cavelike chimney on the right side of the ridge, perhaps 100 feet up from the actual base of the ridge. Climb up, inside the cave, until an exit can be negotiated around the lip of an overhang. Continue up a groove to the ridge and set a belay. The next two fifth-class leads followed by two fourth-class leads continue up the ridge to a steep wall. Climb the obvious chimney/gully which goes up the central portion of the wall and continue up the ridge. The last pitch skirts the final difficulties by following smooth slabs to the right of the main ridgeline. Several hundred feet of scrambling leading to the summit finish the climb.

Route 3, Sun Dog, III, 5.7. Six pitches plus 300 feet of third class. Quality of rock varies from poor to good. Begin the climb on the southwest face about 200 feet from the base of the south ridge just below a small 20-foot flake. Climb up the flake and traverse right at the top of the flake (5.7) to easier rock. A nice little belay bench lies above. The second pitch begins up an off-width crack on the left to a short headwall with an over-

Hail Peak. Photo by David Benyak.

hanging dihedral on the right. Pass the headwall on the left then move back right to a bulging crack just above the headwall. Climb the crack to a good-sized ledge and belay. The third lead climbs directly up and left from the tree just below the ledge. Follow a diagonal crack left to an overhanging flake and chimney to the top of the flake. Move up and left from the flake (5.7) traversing to a small ledge. Jam up a thick flake on the left to a crack below a bulge (packs should probably be hauled up this section). Make your way along the crack up and left to a belay stance below an overhang. The fourth lead passes the overhang on the right and continues up one of several routes to the base of a wide chimney. The final lead follows this chimney (which is also part of the South Ridge Route) to the summit.

Route 4, Chockstone Chimney, II, 5.7. Six pitches plus 300 feet of third class. Quality of rock varies from poor to good. This climb is located on the southwest face of Hail Peak. It begins from an open, rocky area approximately 300 feet south of the ridge which divides the southwest face from the northwest face. Look for a large gully about 200 feet up the rock. Third class a 40-foot crack then scramble over some blocks and bushes to a short right-facing dihedral which contains two side-by-side, fist-width cracks. The first pitch begins here. Climb the dihedral to a grassy ledge then scramble to the base of the gully. Follow the path of least resistance up to a large ledge. More scrambling leads to the belay for the second pitch. From this point climb up and right and then up around a blocky corner. Continue up past several ledges and belay from a tree. The third and crux lead goes straight up to the base of an overhanging buttress. Traverse left below the overhang to the lower portion of the chockstone-filled chimney and belay below the first chockstone. The next two leads continue up the chimney then up a smaller chimney to the left and on up to the south ridge. The final fifth-class pitch climbs a smooth dome and joins the South Ridge Route below an overhang. Pass the overhang on the right and belay. Third or fourth class the rest of the way to the summit.

Route 5, Wildcat, IV, 5.6., A1. Eight fifth-class pitches, one aid pitch, and about 200 feet of third class. Quality of rock varies from poor to good. The climb begins with the same 40-foot third-class crack as Route 4. Immediately at the top of the crack traverse left onto a small rock ledge. Climb 20 feet to a rock ledge and belay. The second lead goes left then up a vertical crack (hard 5.6) to the next belay. The next two pitches continue up and to the left to a large, blank wall with large overhangs forming a dihedral on the right side of the wall. Make your way to the lowest overhang and aid the corner crack (A1) for 50 feet until it terminates. From the top of the aid crack move right and up for 30 feet until a traverse right, around a corner to a small, fractured slab can be made. The first ascent party bivouaced at this slab. The next lead goes up loose rock to an overhang then traverses left and up to the base of a gully formed by a pillar of rock on the right. Continue up the gully to some large chockstones and belay. The eighth pitch climbs to the top of the chockstones then down the opposite side, joining the South Ridge Route. The final pitch plus some scrambling lead to the summit.

Route 6, Pandora's Box, II, 5.6. Eight leads. The first two leads for this route are the same as the first two fifth-class leads for Route 4. Begin the third pitch the same as the third pitch of Route 4 but hand traverse right halfway to the overhanging buttress. Belay from a small, comfortable ledge below a large wall. The fourth lead climbs a few feet above the belay then right to the "Box" overhang which is passed on the left. Climb a 30-

foot crack (5.6) and belay from a ledge at the top of the crack. The next lead (5.6) continues up the Chockstone Chimney and up to the large blocks. The final fifth-class pitch goes up a small dome and around an overhang on the right. Two final fourth-class pitches lead to the summit.

Route 7, After the Gold Rush, II, 5.8. Two sustained fifth-class pitches plus 300 feet of third class. Quality of rock is good to excellent. This climb begins up the Bowling Alley, the ridge that divides the west face. From the top of the Bowling Alley walk south about 20 yards and scramble up some ledges for 30 feet then right and up to a large ledge. A short exposed traverse to the left leads to a smaller ledge with an L-shaped tree above it. Set the first belay at this tree. Climb a crack system to a right-facing dihedral (5.7) and up the crack to the overhanging bulge above. Continue up the crack through the bulge (sustained 5.8) to a small ledge and belay. Begin the next lead up the crack on the left for 30 feet and stem to a ledge on the right. Climb to a short chimney above (a #2 stopper is useful to protect difficult moves below the chimney). From the belay just above the chimney third class the rest of the way to the summit.

Route 8, Northwest Ridge, II, 5.7. Four fifth-class leads plus 200 feet of third class. Quality of rock is fair to poor. This climb starts up a band of dark lichen between red and yellow overhangs located about 50 feet northeast of the base of the northwest ridge. A large block with a horizontal crack marks the first belay stance. The first pitch goes up a short open book (5.6 or 5.7) then to the right around a corner and up to the ridge proper. The second pitch goes up two corners to a slope of big rocks. Scramble 20 feet to a large block at the top of the slope. Climb 15 feet to a short horizontal crack then climb up (5.7) and right to easier rock and a sloping belay stance.

The third lead continues on easy rock to a large ledge above. The fourth lead goes up a gully on the left to a slab covered with loose rock. A thin ledge above the slab runs diagonally from left to right. Climb a crack on the left side of the ledge and set a belay from a tree above. The remainder of the climb involves 200 feet of third- or fourth-class climbing.

Route 9, Poker, II, 5.8. Four fifth-class pitches followed by 150 feet of third class. Good to excellent rock. Begin the climb approximately 200 feet north of the "Bowling Alley" on the west face of Hail Peak. Scramble up easy rock for 75 feet then climb up to a left-facing slot. Traverse left at the slot then up and back to the right on low angle rock above the slot. Continue on steeper rock on the left via a short, steep wall. Climb over easy but rounded rock as far as the rope will allow. If possible begin the next pitch on a ledge below the large overhangs above. The second pitch goes up and left to a large, obvious crack. Climb the crack (5.8) to a small ledge below an open book. Two cracks run vertically up the narrow wall on the right. Climb the cracks, going from one to the other, to a large belay ledge. The next pitch goes up the obvious open book (5.8) which has a ledge at the top. (This ledge is difficult to protect with nuts but a suitable belay can be made higher up.) The last lead goes up waterstained rock to the left of the belay, ending in fourth-class climbing as far as the rope will allow. The second on this pitch can leapfrog and third class his way to the summit.

Descend by downclimbing the ramp on the north side of Hail Peak.

Route 10, Screwy, II, 5.8 or 5.9. Two pitches. Quality of rock is fair. Protection is fair. This route goes up the west face rappel route on Hail Peak. From the top of the Bowling Alley, scramble up small ledges to the south then traverse up and right, to a good-sized ledge. The climb starts up a crack at the left of this ledge. (Route 7 starts about 30 feet farther to the left). Climb the crack to a bulging block 20 feet above the ledge. Continue up and right along a crack (5.9?) which gradually steepens and eventually begins to overhang. At one point it is necessary to exit left to a horizontal flake and then climb up and right, back into the crack. Continue up the crack to easier climbing, then scramble up to a tree and belay.

Scramble up a gully then climb a crack on the right to the summit ridge. Third class to the summit proper.

Route 11, West Face Direct, III, 5.8. Six pitches. Quality of rock is mostly excellent. Protection is good. This climb was first done in 1966 and was not repeated until 10 years later when it was climbed free. The second ascent party furnished this route description.

Approach from the crest. About 100 yards south of the northwest ridge of Hail Peak is a dead tree which marks the start of the climb. Scramble up to the tree and then climb straight up, keeping just right of some overhangs. Climb a short corner to a narrow ledge situated above the overhangs. Climb a vertical crack (5.7) 60 feet to a right-sloping belay ledge. The second lead traverses right above the belay ledge to a lieback up a solid flake. From the top of the flake take one of two routes to the obvious tree above and belay just south of the tree. The third and crux pitch follows a crack above the tree for 30 feet then traverses left to another crack in an open book. Jam and stem (5.8) up the crack until you can accomplish a traverse right onto two rock knobs. Continue up and left to a belay stance at or just below a ledge. From the ledge, the next pitch goes up the easy-looking wall on the left. Near the top of the wall climb a crack (5.7–5.8) which runs through a bulge, past a nest of three pitons, and belay above the bulge. The fifth lead starts by climbing an easy section of undercut rock. Scramble up to a block-filled crack and climb onto a slab at the top of the crack. Climb a small overhang at the top left of the slab (5.7) and climb over big blocks to a large-diameter tree and belay. Complete the climb by accomplishing one final fourth-class pitch to the summit.

Jawbone

Jawbone is a large rib-like buttress located south of the Summit House just below the limestone ridge. It can be identified by its dual summits when viewed from the west.

Route 1, North Ridge, I, 5.3. Two pitches. Quality of rock is fair but watch for loose rock. Approach by hiking down from the crest ridge south of the upper tram terminal. Rappel into the notch between Jawbone and the crest wall, or downclimb the west face to reach the notch. From the notch, climb directly up the north ridge to the summit. The climb ends with a scramble to the top. You can add a Tyrolean traverse across the notch.

Route 2, B.J., 5.7, A0. Four pitches. Quality of rock is good but with some loose rock—mostly on the first pitch. Protection is good.

Start at the base of the slabs located on the southwest end of the Jawbone. From the lowest (south) point on the slabs, scramble 60 feet up to a large fir tree and set a belay just above. The first pitch starts up the obvious 15-foot crack to ledges above. Scramble upward heading for white stains on the large dihedral. Climb a shallow corner for 35 feet to a large block leaning against the wall. Carefully traverse left around the block to a belay ledge. Begin the second pitch by traversing back around the block, then continuing up the large dihedral for 15 feet. Place a small nut in a shallow crack on the face, downclimb a short distance, and tension traverse (A0) about 10 feet to the right until it is possible to freeclimb again. (The tension traverse could probably be freed at 5.8 or 5.9). Continue right to good cracks 30 feet away. Climb the cracks to a suitable belay stance and belay. Continue up the cracks for 40 feet, climb a short, vertical corner, and up the face above. Traverse right along a headwall to a large dihedral, then climb the dihedral to a tree belay 15 feet above. The final pitch goes up a face for 60 feet ending at the south ridge of the Jawbone. From the south ridge, either descend via a series of three rappels into a large gully on the southeast corner of the Jawbone or continue up the ridge to the summit and descend into the notch on the northeast corner.

Route 3, Cactus Flower, III, 5.9. A0 or 5.9. Six pitches including two fourth class.

Begin at the very bottom of the slabs directly below a set of overhangs (one inside the other). The first pitch begins at the bottom of a blank-looking slab. Climb a five-foot face (5.8) to a small tree then make your way up to a large ledge. From the ledge climb up the slab above to a crack system which you follow until it ends. At this point, traverse left to a large, blocky ledge below a blank face. From this ledge climb right, through a bush and around a corner into a chimney below the overhangs. Traverse right, under the overhang and into a layback. From the top of the layback tension traverse 20 feet right to a small, loose block and belay. The fourth pitch angles right, up the face (5.6; difficult to protect with nuts) for a full 165-foot rope length and ends at a huge, tree-covered ledge. Two final easy pitches lead up to the south ridge and then on up the ridge to the summit.

Descend into the notch on the northeast corner.

Route 4, Viva la Revolución, III, 5.7. Climb the huge

Jawbone. Photo by David Benyak.

concave west face immediately east of El Bandarillo with four pitches up its middle. Each pitch gets steeper. On the last pitch leave the central gully that you have been ascending and climb a steep book that is to the left about 15 feet. This takes you to a minor summit of Jawbone. Climb the ridge to the real summit or third class off the lesser one.

Route 5, Double Fantasy, II–III, 5.10. Four pitches. Good rock. This climb is on the south side of the Jawbone and is distinguished by a large, detached block near the end of the technical route. Begin at a grassy area beneath a right-facing corner. Climb up over stacked blocks to a short awkward chimney (5.9) and belay above. The second pitch goes up a chimney system 20 feet to a bush, then follow a crack right, to a bulge, and up to a belay. The third pitch goes to the base of two parallel cracks forming a gully. Climb the crack to the right and belay 60 feet above the crux at the base of a large, detached block. Finish the climb up a crack to the right of the block. The first three pitches are each 5.9 or harder. Friends are useful for this climb.

Pino Wall

Pino Wall is the headwall located immediately east of the Jawbone. To approach drop down west from a saddle in the crest ridge just south of the Summit House to an aspen stand on a saddle between Jawbone and the crest ridge. A scramble to the west along the sharp ridge leading toward Jawbone affords a good view of Pino Wall to the southeast. From the aspen saddle, drop south down a steep couloir to the base of the wall.

Route 1, Pino Wall Route, II, 5.7 or 5.8. Five pitches. Quality of rock is generally very good with good protection using nuts throughout. Start at the base of an obvious, left-facing, black-stained dihedral toward the north end of Pino Wall. Ascend the dihedral to its top, escaping it via a crack on the left. Scramble up a scree to a ledge with several large trees and belay. Climb straight up from the ledge in a shallow crack to a small horn. Step right, then ascend up and left to a wide crack just below a small tree. From the tree, climb the face above for 50 feet to the base of a right-facing dihedral. Belay just below the dihedral on a cozy, flat stance to the right. Ascend the dihedral (some good jamming) until the crack ends. Traverse right to a small left-facing book with a good crack. Climb this book and then the face above on good cracks. Traverse left on broken terrain to the original right-facing dihedral and belay from a good stance in the corner. Continue straight up the dihedral for 30 feet to a large chockstone which is turned to the right with a mantle. Ascend the dihedral above to just below a steep, yellow headwall and traverse right then up an easy face to a spacious ledge and belay. Finish up easy rock for 30 feet to the summit.

El Diente

El Diente (the tooth) is the small pinnacle located on the lower south end of the Jawbone buttress.

Route 1, South Ridge, I, 5.5. One pitch. From the base of El Diente climb directly up the ridge over a series of ledges until you reach the summit. From the top descend to the notch on the north side and either rappel down the west side of the notch or continue up the ridge to the summit of Jawbone.

El Bandarillo

This is the small, sharp pinnacle lying to the northwest and below Jawbone's summit.

Route 1, 5.2? One pitch. Begin this climb up the north face then angle right to the southwest corner. Climb up the corner to the small summit block.

South Peak Buttresses

The South Peak Buttresses are four prominent buttresses located just below the ridgeline south of South Sandia Peak. The approach is particularly long from any direction but is probably easiest by hiking up Three Gun Spring Trail and then scrambling across to the buttresses. The buttresses are numbered one through four starting with the buttress to the north.

Route 1, Eagles Nest, I, 5.5. Three pitches. From the bottom of the prominent crescent-shaped overhang on the west face of the second buttress from the north, climb diagonally to the right by way of a chimney to a belay position under the overhang. Escape right to a ledge containing a large nest. Continue to the right and then up to a second belay. The finish is a fourth-class scramble to the top.

Route 2, Second Buttress-North Side, II, 5.4. Quality of rock is fair to good. Three leads of roped climbing. Climb up the gully north of the second buttress to the base of the northwest corner and traverse around to the north up mossy slabs nearly halfway to the top. It is at this point that the roped climbing begins. Three short leads up the north face gain the summit.

Route 3, Third Buttress, II, 5.4. Four roped pitches. Quality of rock is fair. Begin the climb at the base of the middle west face of the third buttress from the north and angle right on grassy ledges to the south ridge. Angle across the southeast face and take any of several possible routes to the top. The original route took a fourth-class gully up the south face to the top but other

Bob Kyrlach on Eagles Nest, South Peak buttresses. Photo by Carl Smith.

routes as hard as 5.7 are possible. Overall the route is not well defined. Note the debris from an old airplane crash located on the slopes just below the third buttress.

Route 4, Wrolstad's Wall, I, 5.6. One pitch. This climb is located on the southernmost buttress. Begin near the bottom of the couloir which separates the third buttress from the wall. Climb over a flake and angle to the right. Step around a corner and climb a crack 20 feet to a ledge. Angle right again to a larger ledge and scramble to the top of the wall.

PRACTICE AREAS

Embudo Canyon

Reach this area using the approach given for the Embudo Trail. Most of the boulder problems are located within a few hundred feet up the canyon from the artificial waterfall. The boulder problems are located on both sides of the canyon and are mostly short enough to eliminate the need for a rope.

Juan Tabo Canyon

This is a favorite practice area for the Mountain Club Climbing Schools. Approach by way of the Piedra Lisa Spring Trail. When the trail crosses the Juan Tabo Arroyo, hike south down the arroyo. Most of the practice climbing is located around one-half mile down the arroyo from the trail crossing. There are both short boulder problems and longer top-rope climbs. A shortcut to this area can be taken by hiking west to the arroyo from the small parking area across the road from the entrance to the Juan Tabo Picnic Area.

Embudito Canyon

To reach this area follow the Embudito Trail to where the canyon begins to narrow down and the walls become well defined. A number of short climbs can be top-roped on both sides of the canyon. These climbs require some scrambling.

Tijeras Canyon

Approach this area by traveling east on Central Avenue and then turning south onto the service road that runs in from off the Western Skies Motel. Follow this road east past the Four Hills turnoff and then several hundred feet farther on until you see some low, scattered adobe ruins off to the right of the road. Turn right and drive south past these ruins (once called Beavertown) and follow one of several rough dirt roads down into the arroyo. The practice climbing is done on the cliffs which can be seen on the south side of the canyon. One large section is particularly obvious. It can be top-roped and provides a number of routes with some good practice at delicate faceclimbing.

Other Areas

The White Wash just north of Embudo Canyon and U Mound at the end of Lomas have some good top-rope problems. Also, one can top-rope on the limestone rim that runs along the crest and is quite solid in places. In fact, virtually every canyon along the entire west face of the Sandias offers some type of climbing or bouldering. The only thing that keeps many of these from being popular practice areas is poor accessibility.

APPENDIX A

Weather Means and Extremes by Month (1954–1965)
for Sandia Crest Weather Station (10,625 ft.)
Furnished by U.S. Department of Commerce, Weather Bureau

Month	Temperature (°F)						Precipitation Totals (Inches)			
	Mean		Extremes					Snow, sleet		
									Maximum	
	Avg. Max.	Avg. Min.	High	Year	Low	Year	Mean	Mean	Mo.	Year
Jan.	17.2	13.9	47	1959	−15	1962	1.75	20.0	40.5	1960
Feb.	18.2	14.3	46	1957	−12	1963*	1.77	23.5	60.3	1964
March	31.5	16.7	56	1959	−7	1965	2.32	22.9	67.9	1958
April	42.4	24.3	60	1965	−2	1955	1.18	10.4	34.5	1958
May	53.7	34.6	70	1958	12	1965	.99	2.3	7.5	1964
June	64.6	43.8	76	1957	29	1955	.78	.1	1.0	1965
July	66.8	47.4	80	1958	29	1962	2.85	.1	1.0	1955
Aug.	63.6	46.7	77	1961	37	1960	3.19	0	0	-
Sept.	58.4	41.9	71	1958	19	1965	1.61	.1	1.0	1961
Oct.	48.9	34.1	62	1958	11	1958	1.94	6.0	24.0	1960
Nov.	36.8	22.7	53	1962	−6	1957	1.25	8.3	27.6	1957
Dec.	30.3	17.0	50	1965	−19	1961	2.43	24.6	53.0	1959

APPENDIX B

Birds of the Sandia Mountains

LEGEND: Abundance
A—Abundant
C—Common
UC—Uncommon
R—Rare: One or two sightings

Status R—Resident
T—Transient
WR—Winter Resident
SR—Summer Resident

CHICKADEES, NUTHATCHES
Black-capped Chickadee R T
Mountain Chickadee A R
Plain Titmouse C R
Bushtit C R
White-breasted Nuthatch C R
Red-breasted Nuthatch C R

Pygmy Nuthatch C R
Brown Creeper UC R
Dipper R

CUCKOOS, ROADRUNNER
Yellow-billed Cuckoo R T
Roadrunner UC R

CRANES, RAILS
Sandhill Crane R T
American Coot R T

DUCKS
Mallard
American Wigeon R T
Green-winged Teal R T
Cinnamon Teal R T
Northern Shoveler
Ring-necked Duck R T

FINCHES, SPARROWS
Rose-breasted Grosbeak R T
Black-headed Grosbeak A SR
Blue Grosbeak UC SR
Indigo Bunting UC SR
Lazuli Bunting UC SR
Evening Grosbeak C WR
Cassin's Finch C WR
House Finch C R
Pine Grosbeak R T
Gray-crowned Rosy Finch R WR
Pine Siskin A R
American Goldfinch R T
Lesser Goldfinch C SR
Red Crossbill UC R
Green-tailed Towhee C SR
Rufous-sided Towhee C SR
Brown Towhee CR
Lark Sparrow UC SR
Rufous-crowned Sparrow UC R
Black-throated Sparrow C SR

Sage Sparrow R R
Dark-eyed Junco, Slate-colored Race UC WR
Dark-eyed Junco, Oregon Race A WR
Gray-headed Junco A R
Chipping Sparrow A SR
Clay-colored Sparrow R T
Brewer's Sparrow R T
Black-chinned Sparrow UC SR
Harris' Sparrow R T
White-crowned Sparrow C WR
Golden-crowned Sparrow R T
Fox Sparrow R T
Lincoln's Sparrow UC T
Song Sparrow UC WR
Chestnut-collared Longspur R T

FLYCATCHERS
Western Kingbird R T
Cassin's Kingbird C SR
Ash-throated Flycatcher C SR
Eastern Phoebe R T
Black Phoebe R T
Say's Phoebe R T
Willow Flycatcher R T
Hammond's Flycatcher UC SR
Dusky Flycatcher R T
Gray Flycatcher R T
Western Flycatcher C SR
Western Wood Peewee C SR
Olive-sided Flycatcher C SR

GNATCATCHERS, KINGLETS
Blue-gray Gnatcatcher C SR
Golden-crowned Kinglet UC T
Ruby-crowned Kinglet C R

GOATSUCKERS
Whip-poor-will R T
Poor-will UC SR
Common Nighthawk C SR

GROUSE
Blue R R

HAWK, EAGLES
Goshawk UC R
Sharp-shinned Hawk UC R
Cooper's Hawk UC R
Red-tailed Hawk UC
Swainson's Hawk R T
Ferruginous Hawk R T
Rough-legged Hawk R T
Golden Eagle UC R
Bald Eagle R T
Mark Hawk R T
Osprey R T
Prairie Falcon UC R
Peregrine Falcon R T
Merlin R T
American Kestrel UC R

HERON
Black-crowned Night R T

HUMMINGBIRDS
Black-chinned C SR
Broad-tailed A SR
Rufous C T
Calliope UC T
Rivoli's R T

JAYS, MAGPIES, CROWS
Blue Jay R T
Steller's Jay C R
Scrub Jay C R
Black-billed Magpie R T
Common Raven C R
Common Crow C R
Pinon Jay C R
Clark's Nutcracker UC R

LARKS
Horned C R

MEADOWLARKS, BLACKBIRDS, ORIOLES
Western Meadowlark UC R
Scott's Oriole UC SR
Northern Oriole, Baltimore Race R T
Northern Oriole, Bullock's Race UC SR
Brown-headed Cowbird C R

MIMICS AND THRUSHES
Mockingbird C SR
Gray Catbird R T
Brown Thrasher R T
Curved-billed Thrasher UC R
Crissal Thrasher UC R
Sage Thrasher UC WR
American Robin A R
Hermit Thrush C R
Swainson's Thrush R T
Eastern Bluebird R T/WR
Western Bluebird C R
Mountain Bluebird C R
Townsend's Solitaire C R

OWLS
Screech R R
Flammulated R DR
Great Horned C R
Pygmy UC R
Spotted R R
Saw-Whet R?

PIPIT, WAXWINGS
Water Pipit R T
Bohemian Waxwing R T
Cedar Waxwing UC T/WR

QUAIL
Scaled C R

SANDPIPERS AND SNIPE
Common Snipe R T
Solitary Sandpiper R T
SPOTTED SANDPIPER R T

SHRIKES, STARLINGS
Northern Shrike R T
Loggerhead Shrike C R
Starling UC R

SWALLOWS
Violet-Green A SR
Tree UC T
Barn C SR

SWIFTS
White-throated C SR
Tanagers
Western C SR
Scarlet R T
Hepatic R SR
Summer R T ?

TURKEY
Merriam's R R

WEAVER FINCH
House Sparrow C R

WOOD WARBLERS
Black-and-White UC T
Tennessee R T
Orange-crowned C SR
Nashville R T
Virginia's C SR
Northern Parula R T
Yellow UC T
Magnolia R T
Black-throated Blue R T
Yellow-rumped, Myrtle Race UC T
Yellow-rumped, Audubon's Race A SR
Black-throated Gray UC SR
Townsend's UC T
Grace's C SR
Chestnut-sided R T
Ovenbird R T

Northern Waterthrush R T
MacGillivray's C SR
Common Yellowthroat R T
Yellow-breasted Chat UC SR
Hooded R T
Wilson's C T
American Redstart R T

WOODPECKERS
Common Flicker, Yellow-shafted Race R T
Common Flicker, Red-shafted Race A R
Lewis' UC T
Yellow-bellied Sapsucker C SR
Williamson's Sapsucker C SR
Hairy Woodpecker C R
Downy Woodpecker C R
Ladder-backed Woodpecker C R
Northern Three-toed Woodpecker R R

WRENS
House C SR
Winter R T
Bewick's C R
Carolina R
Canon C R
Rock C R

VIREOS
Solitary C SR
Red-eyed R T
Warbling C SR

VULTURES
Turkey C SR

PIGEONS, DOVES
Band-tailer Pigeon C R
Mourning Dove C SR

SUGGESTED LOCATIONS FOR BIRD STUDY IN THE SANDIAS

Spruce Fir Forest (Hudsonian Zone)	Kiwanis Meadow Upper tram terminal area
Douglas Fir Forest (Canadian Zone)	Capulin Springs, Tree Springs
Ponderosa Pine Forest (Transition Zone)	Doc Long Picnic Area, Cienega Canyon
Pinon-Juniper Woodland (Upper Sonoran Zone)	Juan Tabo Canyon Area

APPENDIX C

Checklist of Mammals of the Sandia Mountains

INSECT EATERS

Vagrant Shrew, *Sorex vagrans*
Dwarf Shrew, *Sorex nanus*
Merriam's Shrew, *Sorex meriami*

BATS

Fringes Myotis, *Myotis thysanodes*
Little Brown Myotis, *Myotis lucifugus*
Keen Myotis, *Myotis keeni*
Long-legged Myotis, *Myotis volans*
Small-footed Myotis, *Myotis subulatus*
Silver-haired Bat, *Lasionycteris noctinagans*
Hoary Bat, *Lasiurus cinereus*
Western Big-eared Bat, *Pecotus townsendi*

Pallid Bat, *Antrozous pallidus*
Mexican Freetail Bat, *Tadarida brasiliensis*

FLESH-EATERS

Black Bear, *Ursus americanus*
Raccoon, *Procyon lotor*
Ringtailed Cat, *Bassariscus astutus*
Long-tailed Weasel, *Mustela frenata*
Spotted Skunk, *Spilogale putorius*
Striped Skunk, *Mephitis mephitis*
Hog-nosed Skunk, *Conepatus leuconotus*
Badger, *Taxidea taxus*
Coyote, *Canis latrans*
Wolf (Lobo), *Canis lupus*
Swift Fox, *Vulpes velox*
Gray Fox, *Urocyon cinereoargenteus*
Mountain Lion, *Felis concolor*
Bobcat, *Lynx rufus*

GNAWING MAMMALS

Gunnison (White-tailed) Prairie Dog, *Cynomys gunnisoni*
Ground Squirrel, *Cittelus*
Gray-tailed Antelope Ground Squirrel, *Citellus interpres*
Rock Squirrel, *Citellus variegatus*
Colorado Chipmunk, *Eutamias quadrivittatus*
Least Chipmunk, *Eutamias minimus*
Spruce Squirrel, *Tamiasciurus hudsonicus*
Tassel-eared (Abert) Squirrel, *Sciurus aberti*
Southwestern Pocket Gopher, *Thomomys bottae*
Mexican Pocket Gopher, *Cratogeomys castonops*
Silky Pocket Mouse, *Perognathus flavus*
Hispid Pocket Mouse, *Perognathus hispidus*
Bannertail Kangaroo Rat, *Dipodomys spectabilis*
Ord Kangaroo Rat, *Dipodomys ordi*
Western Harvest Mouse, *Reithrodontomys megalotis*

White-footed Mouse, *Peromyscus leucopus*
Deer Mouse, *Peromyscus maniculatus*
Brush Mouse, *Peromyscus boylei*
Pinyon Mouse, *Peromyscus truei*
Rock Mouse, *Peromyscus difficilis*
Northern Grasshopper Mouse, *Onychomys leucogaster*
White-throated Woodrat, *Neotoma albigula*
Southern Plains Woodrat, *Neotoma micropus*
Mexican Woodrat, *Neotoma mexicana*
Longtail Vole, *Microtus longicaudus*
Porcupine, *Erethizon dorsatun*

HARES AND RABBITS

Black-tailed Jackrabbit, *Lepus clifornicus*
Desert Cottontail, *Sylvilagus auduboni*
Eastern Cottontail, *Sylvilagus floridanus*

HOOFED ANIMALS

Mule Deer, *Odocoileus hemionus*
Rocky Mountain Bighorn Sheep, *Ovis canadensis*

APPENDIX D

Reptiles and Amphibians of the Sandia Mountains

AMPHIBIANS

Tiger Salamander, *Ambystomids tigrinum*
Great Basin Spadefoot, *Scaphiopus intermontanus*
Woodhouse's Toad, *Bufo woodhousei*
Red-spotted Toad, *Bufo punctatus*
Leopard Frog, *Rana pipiens*
Chorus Frog, *Pseudacris trisceriata*

LIZARDS

Great Plains Skink, *Eumeces obsoletus*
Many-lined Skink, *Eumeces multivirgatus gaigei*
Spotted Whiptail, *Cnemidophorus exsanguis*
Little Striped Whiptail, *Cnemidophorus inoratus heptagrammus*

New Mexico Whiptail, *Cnemidophorus neomexicanus*
Checkered Whiptail, *Cnemidophorus resselatus tesselatus*
Plateau Whiptail, *Cnemidophorus velox*
Western Collard Lizard, *Crotophytus collaris baileyi*
Speckled Earless Lizard, *Holbrookia maculata approximans*
Mountain Short-horned Lizard, *Phrynosoma douglassi hernandesi*
Round-tailed Horned Lizard, *Phrynosoma modestum*
Northern Plateau Lizard, *Sceloporus undulatus elongatus*
Northern Side-blotched Lizard, *Uta stansburiana stansburiana*
Easter Tree Lizard, *Urosaurus ornatus ornatus*

SNAKES

New Mexico Blink Snake, *Leptotyphlops dulcis dissectus*
Western Black-necked Garter Snake, *Thamnophis crytopsis crytopsis*
Wandering Garter Snake, *Thamnophis elegans vagrans*
Dusty Hognose Snake, *Heterodon nasicus gloydi*
Prairie Ring-neck Snake, *Diadophis punctatus arnyi*
Pink Coachwhip, *Masticophis taeniatus taeniatus*
Mountain Patch-nosed Snake, *Salvadora graphamiae grahamiae*
Great Basin Gopher Snake, *Pituophis melanoleucus deserticola*
Central Plains Milk Snake, *Lampropeltis doliata gentilis*
Desert Long-nosed Snake, *Rhinocheilus lecontei clarus*
Mesa Verde Night Snake, *Hypsiglena torquata loreala*
Plains Black-headed Snake, *Tantilla nigriceps nigriceps*
Western Diamondback Rattlesnake, *Crotalus atrox*
Northern Black-tailed Rattlesnake, *Crotalus molussus molussus*
Prairie Rattlesnake, *Crotalus viridis viridis*

TURTLES

Ornate Box Turtle, *Terrapene ornata luteola*

TOTAL SPECIES—39

APPENDIX E

LIST OF FIRST ASCENTS

BEASTIE:
Zig Zag—Jack and LaDonna Kutz, Paul Wohit, Pete Skaates;
    October 1966

LADY:
Northeast Face—Unknown

BIG PIG:
East Side—Unknown
North Side—Unknown
West Wide—Unknown

MIDDLE PIG:
East Face—Unknown
South Face—Unknown

LOBO:
Northwest Face—Jack and LaDonna Kutz; May 1966

DEL AGUA SPIRE:
Southeast Ridge—Bob Kyrlach and Pete Skaates; 1968
North Face—Jack and LaDonna Kutz, Bob Kyrlach, Pete
  Skaates, Gary Holcum; November 1964.

SHIELD:
Knife Edge—Unknown
Route 2—Jack and LaDonna Kutz, Bob Kyrlach, Pete Skaates,
  Paul Wohlt, Dave Logan; May 1966
Route 3—Jack and LaDonna Kutz, Paul Wohlt, Goedecke;
  September 1969
Route 4—Dick Ingraham, Bob Kyrlach, Mid-1960s
Standard S Route—Unknown
Route 6—Unknown
Procrastination—Steve Merrill, Steve Schum; July 1970
Smorgasbord—Unknown
North Face—Pete Skaates, Bob Kyrlach; Mid-1960s
Rainbow Route—Mike Roybal, John Mauldin; June 1973
Carrot—Carlos Buhler, Jim Freels; Spring 1975
Chicken Chop Suey—Robbie Baker, Charlie Ware; May 1973
Pickle—John Mauldin, Scott Davis; June 1975
Interrupted Journey—Dave Legits, Jay Evans; July 1975
Slipping Into Darkness—Gary Hicks, Ron Beauchamp; July
  18, 1976. First free ascent—Hans Brede, Peter Prandoni.
Orange Sunshine—Davito Hammack, Rick Meleski; February
  1977.
Superglide—Doug Bridgers, Gary Hicks, Wayne Taylor; May
  1978.
Cowboy's Delight—Davito Hammack, Rick Meleski; 1978
Rainbow Dancer—Peter Prandoni, Doug Bridgers; 1979

UNM SPIRE:
Saddle Route—Unknown
Standard South Ridge Route—Unknown
Southwest Corner—Doug Bridgers, Kathy Kocon, Rick
  Meleski; March 18, 1974.
East Face—Unknown
West Face to South Ridge—Unknown

THE PROW:

Southeast Ridge—Thunderbird Mt. Club; 1948 (first recorded ascent)

South Face—Unknown

Bird Ridge—Kurt Groepler, Scott Dye; June 14, 1965

Northwest Ridge—Unknown

Hanging Sling Buttress—Gary Hicks, Florian Walchak; November 10, 1974

NEEDLE:

East Saddle—William Elam and companion(s); 1944. This is the first recorded ascent of the needle although there were undoubtedly earlier ascents.

East Saddle Caves—Jack Kutz, Terry Kutz, Mike Stroud, Joan Pease; June 1970

Southeast Ridge—Unknown

Southwest Ridge—Reed Cundiff, David Hammack; June 27, 1959

Route 5—Bob Kyrlach, Dan Petersen; 1969

Hoy's Chimney—Bill Hoy and companion(s); date unknown

Northwest Ridge—Unknown

Upper West Face Direct—Unknown

Upper West Face Variation—Unknown

TOMBSTONE:

West Face Traverse—Keith Wrolstad, Nelson Gillis, Larry Kline; May 1970

North Face—Mike Dennis, Charlie Ware; May 10, 1971

West Face-Left Side—Mike Dennis, Charlie Ware, June 18, 1971

West Face Direct—Mike Dennis, Charlie Ware; May 17, 1971

Feats Don't Fail Me Now (North Face)—Peter Prandoni and companion, Fall 1976

KNIFE BLADE:

Crack of Black—Charlie Ware, Mike Dennis; June 12, 1972

MUMMY:

Route 1—Bob Kyrlach and companion; date unknown

CASTLE:

Upper South Ridge—Larry Kline, Keith Wrolstad, Nelson Gillis; July 1970

Crujida De La Reina—Rick Meleski, Davito Hammack; March 1976

Nada Wall—Rick Meleski, Davito Hammack; Fall 1976

Crujida Puta—Davito Hammack, Rick Meleski; Fall 1976

EL TECOLOTE:

Quack—Mike Roybal, Peter Prandoni

Crystal Corner—Gary Hicks, Wayne Taylor; September 1980

CAKE:

North Face—Bob Kyrlach, Jack and LaDonna Kutz, Pete Skaates; October 1965

West Face Traverse—Unknown

Corkscrew—Jack and LaDonna Kutz, Pete Skaates, Paul Wohlt; March 1967

South Couloir—Bob Kyrlach, Jack and LaDonna Kutz, Degenhardt; July 1969

A Piece of Cake—Hessing, Roybal; March 1971

CANDLE:

Southeast Corner—Frank White, Joe Olonia; Late 1960s

West Face Direct—Keith Wrolstad, Nelson Gillis, Larry Kline; June 1969

West Face Escape—Nelson Gillis, Keith Wrolstad, Larry Kline; 1968

North Face—Bill Isenhower, Mike Roybal; July 1970

MURALLA GRANDE:

La Selva Route—Rick Meleski, Doug Bridgers; June 1974

Clark's Cramps—Mike Roybal, Clark Gray; 1973

Labor Day Route—John Allen, Paul Smith; September 3, 1971

Warpy Moople—Mike Roybal, Peter Prandoni; August 1975

Short But Thin—Prandoni, McFarland; July 1975

Masochist Variant—Peter Prandoni, Doug Bridgers; July 1975

Fantasia—Ron Beauchamp, Gary Hicks; August 17, 1975

Out to Lunch—Doug Bridgers, Peter Prandoni; July 1976.

First free ascent—Gary Hicks, Davito Hammack, Doug Bridgers; July 1979.

The Second Coming—Joe Darriau, Thad Meyerriecks; November, 1976

Dire Straights—Mark Leonard, Mark Dalen; June 1980

Bunghole Borer—Mark Leonard, Mike Smith; October 1979

After Lunch—Peter Prandoni and companion.

LOOKOUT:

South Ridge—Jack and LaDonna Kutz, Bob Kyrlach, Lilly Rendt, Dan Petersen; September 1967

North Ridge—Peter Skaates, Rich Berlint; date unknown

CHIMNEY:

East Ridge—Unknown

North Face Traverse—Unknown

West Side—Keith Wrolstad, Larry Kline; October 1969

North To Upper West Face—Unknown

Rocky Raccoon—Charlie Ware, Mike Hill, John Allen; Spring 1975

North Face Direct—Unknown

Another Imbecile Variant—Munroe, Roybal; February 1971

Schum's Delight—Steve Schum, Steve Merrill; 1970

SENTINEL:

West Face—Unknown

Lost Ledge—Steve Merrill, Larry Kline; June 1970

North Ridge—Keith Wrolstad, Nelson Gillis, Selleck; June 1970

Lettuce Patch—Mike Hill, Bob Hammond; Spring 1976

LOWER LA CUEVA CANYON:

The Incher—Paul Horak, Mark Dalen; 1975

Gemstone—Gary Hicks, Jim Fuge; June 8, 1974.

Markingstone—Paul Horak, Mark Dalen; October 1976.

Seamingly Hard—Gary Hicks (solo); September 1979.

Birthday Cake—Gary Hicks, R. McCaniff; July 1981

THE PULPIT:

Southeast Ridge—Unknown

Cave Route—Bill Isenhower, Mike Roybal, Clark Gray; May 1970.

Direct Variation—Spin Shaffer, Jay Abeyta; October 1980.

Waterstains—Unknown

Poontang—Davito Hammack, Rick Meleski; Fall, 1976

Snake Eyes—Bruce Doeren, Mark Leonard; July 1981.

LOST SPECTACLE:

Notch to West Face—Unknown

Notch Direct—Unknown

South Ridge—Unknown

Mentally Vacuous Frippery—Mike Roybal, John Mauldin; August 1973

Moonlight Serenade—Jim Freels, Carlos Buhler; Spring 1975

YATAGHAN:

Southeast Face—Reed Cundiff, David Hammack; October 1, 1960

East Face Variation—Nelson Gillis; Keith Wrolstad, June 1968

The Happy Gnome (West Face)—Rick Meleski, Doug Bridgers; 1974

West Face Variation—Peter Prandoni, Greg McFarland; Summer 1976

Blood on the Blade—David Baltz, Mark Leonard, Paul Horak; July 1979

FROG:

West Ridge—Reed Cundiff, David Hammack, August 27, 1960

CHAOS CRAG:

Southwest Face—Reed Cundiff, David Hammack; September 17, 1960

Metamorphosis—Rick Meleski, Doug Bridgers; 1974

Duck Soup—Rick Meleski, Doug Bridgers; Summer 1976. First free ascent by Paul Horak, Mark Dalen, and Andrew Embick; April 1977.

EL PAISANO:

El Paisano—Wayne Taylor, Sue Butcher; October 1980

MEXICAN BREAKFAST:
Mexican Breakfast Crack—Doug Bridgers, Wayne Taylor; June 1974
Tarantula—Peter Prandoni, Jenny McKernan; Summer 1976

TORREON:
Mountain Momma—Dennis Udall, Dirk VanWinkle; April 1977
Sorcerer's Apprentice—Peter Prandoni, Gary Hicks, Doug Bridgers; August 1979.
Wizard of Odd—Mike Roybal, Peter Prandoni, Doug Bridgers; 1980
Bitch's Brew—Peter Prandoni, Ron Beauchamp; September 1981

RAT'S ROCK:
Lost Hole—Gary Hicks, Florian Walchak; September 1, 1975
Bombs Away—Mark Leonard, Gary Hicks; September 1979
Behind Blue Eyes—Mark Leonard, Mike Smith; October 1979
FIN:
Exhibition Wall—Nelson Gillis, Larry Kline; August 1969.
    First free ascent by Mike Roybal and Peter Prandoni; 1976.
North Ridge—Mark Dalen, Larry Coats; 1975

DONALD DUCK:
Northeast Corner—Larry Kline, Keith Wrolstad; June 1969

FIRE HYDRANT:
Northwest Face—Keith Wrolstad, Steve Merrill, Larry Kline; July 1970

PAIRED POLE PILLARS:
North Gully—Nelson Gillis, Larry Kline; August 1968
Northwest Face—Larry Kline, Nelson Gillis; August 1968
Southeast Corner—Unknown
Northeast Corner—Keith Wrolstad, Larry Kline; June 1969
Plimsolls—Mark Leonard, Bruce Doeren; July 1979

ESTRELLITA:
Route 1—Davito Hammack, Rick Meleski, 1976

REDEEMER:
Route 1—Unknown
Occasional Freshman—Carlos Buhler, Sue Giller; Spring 1974
Northwest Corner—Carlos Buhler and companion; Fall 1974

THUMB:
Southeast Ridge—Unknown
East Face—Unknown
East Face Direct—David Hammack, Don Lundergan; 1960
North Summit Direct—Reed Cundiff, David Hammack; 1960
Northwest Ridge—Unknown
Southwest Chimney—Unknown
Route 7—Unknown
Route 8—Unknown
Waterstains Route—Davito Hammack, Dan Buck, Cliff
    Thomas; 1974
Muralla Blanca—Doug Bridgers, Kathy Kocon, Rick Meleski;
    April 28, 1974. First free ascent—Erik Keto, Ron Beau-
    champ; August 1977
Zonker's Folly—Doug Bridgers, Rick Meleski; April 1974
Aviary Ort Overhangs—Doug Bridgers, Rick Meleski; July
    1975

HOLE IN THE WALL:
Miss Piggy—Mike Hill, Norm Wendell; 1980

TRIDENTS:
Potwana—Wayne Taylor, Curt Verplough; July 1974
Lost Line—Wayne Taylor, Gary Hicks; August 1975
5.10 Squirrel—Wayne Taylor, Mark Dalen; October 1975
Narrow Escape—Wayne Taylor, Gordon Darbro; November
    1976
Misty Ridge—Wayne Taylor, Curt Verploegh; July 1977
Debauchers' Deluxe—Wayne Taylor, John Dillon; 1980

YUCCA FLOWER TOWER:
Route 1—Charles Ware, Mark Dalen; February 1977

LA VISTA:
La Vista—Jim Fuge, Gary Hicks; September 1976

Against the Wind—Mark Leonard, Kathy Kocon-Hicks; May 1980

THE POINT:
Power of Words—Mark Leonard, Mark Dalen; June 1980
Sid Vicious: David Baltz, Mark Leonard; 1980

ECHO CANYON, MISCELLANEOUS:
Westeron Winde—Mark Dalen, Mark Leonard; July 1980
Fear of Flying—Wayne Taylor, Cayce Weber; January 1981
Increasingly Dred—Mike Smith (solo); November 1981

EGO BOOST:
Southeast Ridge—Gary Hicks, Jay Stagnone; March 26, 1974
Hang Glide—Gary Hicks, Florian Walchak, Jim Fuge; May 25, 1974
Diagonal—Gary Hicks, Jim Fuge; October 5, 1975

ALIOTH:
Alioth's Nose—Dan Buck, Davito Hammack; 1975
East Ridge—Dan Buck, Davito Hammack; 1975
West Chimney—Dan Buck, Davito Hammack; 1975
Block Ridge Edge—Dan Buck, Davito Hammack; 1975
Last Goodby—Mark Leonard, Kathy Kocon-Hicks, Gary Hicks; 1980.

HAIL PEAK:
North Ramp—Unknown
Windy Ridge—Jay Evans, Carlos Buhler; Spring 1974
Sun Dog—Florian Walchak, Gary Hicks; August 31, 1974
Chockstone Chimney—Jim Fuge, Gary Hicks; September 22, 1974
Wildcat—Gary Hicks, Florian Walchak; May 10-11, 1974
Pandora's Box—Gary Hicks, Steve Jones; July 22, 1975
After the Gold Rush—Ron Beauchamp, Gary Hicks; October 19, 1975
Northwest Ridge—Gary Hicks, Ron Beauchamp; November 9, 1975
Poker—Gary Hicks, Florian Walchak; June 13, 1976

Screwy—Erik Keto, Wayne Taylor, Gary Hicks; August 8, 1976

West Face Direct—Jack Kutz, Paul Wohlt; September 17, 1966. First free ascent—Gary Hicks and Jim Fuge; October 3, 1976

JAWBONE:

North Ridge—Unknown

Cactus Flower—Ken Jonke, Tom Breeze, Dan Roberts; June 13, 1976. First free ascent by Ron Beauchamp and Florian Walchak, February, 1977

B.J.—Ron Beauchamp, Gordon Darbro; 1976

Viva La Revolución—Gordon Darbro, Rick Meleski; 1977

Double Fantasy—Gary Hicks, David Baltz, Mark Leonard; December 1980

PINO WALL:

Pino Wall Route—Gordon Darbro, Ron Beauchamp; March 1976

EL DIENTE:

South Ridge—Unknown

EL BANDARILLO:

Route 1—Jack and LaDonna Kutz; 1966

SOUTH PEAK BUTTRESSES:

Eagles Nest—Nelson Gillis, Keith Wrolstad, Larry Kline; April 1968

Second Buttress-North Side—Don Mattox, Bob Kyrlach, Dan Petersen, John Lowe, Richard Fleming; October 20, 1974

Third Buttress—Keith Wrolstad, Nelson Gillis, Larry Kline; April 1968

Wrolstad's Wall—Keith Wrolstad, Nelson Gillis, Larry Kline; April 1968

BIBLIOGRAPHY

Advanced Rockcraft. By Royal Robbins, La Siesta Press, Glendale Ca., 1971.

Accidents in North American Mountaineering. Published yearly by The American Alpine Club.

Albuquerque: Its Mountains, Valley, Water and Volcanoes. By Vincent C. Kelly, State Bureau of Mines and Mineral Resources, New Mexico Institute of Mining and Technology, Campus Station, Socorro, N.M., 1969.

Basic Rockcraft. By Royal Robbins, La Siesta Press, Glendale, Ca., 1971.

Backpacking—One Step At A Time. By Harvey Manning, Vintage Books, Random House, New York, N.Y., Revised Edition, 1975.

Cross-Country Skiing... By Ned Gillette, The Mountaineers, Seattle, Wash., 1979.

Edible Wild Plants of the Rocky Mountains. By H. D. Harrington, UNM Press, 1967.

Final Environmental Statement—Sandia Mountains—Land Use Plan, Department of Agriculture, Forest Service.

Hypothermia: Killer of the Unprepared. Published by the Mazamas, 909 N.W. Nineteenth Ave., Portland, Oregon, Revised Edition 1975.

Medicine for Mountaineering. Edited by James A. Wilkerson, M.D., Mountaineers, Seattle, Wash., Second Edition 1975.

Mountaineering First Aid. By Dick Mitchell, Mountaineers, Seattle, Wash. 1972.

Mountaineering: The Freedom of the Hills. By the Climbing Committee of the Mountaineers, Edited by Peggy Ferber, Mountaineers, Seattle, Wash., Third Edition 1974.

The New Complete Walker. By Colin Fletcher, Alfred A. Knopf, New York, N.Y., 1975.

Oku Pin, The Sandia Mountains of New Mexico. By James A. Morris, Seven Goats Editions, Albuquerque, N.M., 1980.

Outdoor Living. (A Wilderness Survival Manual). Published by The Tacoma Mountain Rescue Unit, Tacoma, Wash.

Plant Distribution of the Sandia Mountain Area, New Mexico. By James N. Naylor, Thesis, University of New Mexico, 1964.

Ski Touring in Northern New Mexico. By Sam Beard, Adobe Press, Albuquerque, N.M., 1979.

Snowshoeing. By Gene Prater, The Mountaineers, Seattle, Wash., 1974.

Southwestern Trees: A Guide To the Native Species of New Mexico and Arizona. By Elbert L. Little, Jr., Agriculture Handbook No. 9, U.S. Department of Agriculture, Washington, D.C., 1968.

Walking Softly in the Wilderness. By John Hart, Sierra Club Books, San Francisco, Ca., 1977.

INDEX

Tijeras Forest Service Ranger Station, 20, 101
Tijeras Quad, 9
Tombstone, the, 108–10
Tooth. *See* Del Agua Spire; El Diente
Topography, 9
Torreon, 146, 148, 150, 152
Tours, Forest Service, 18
Trail: corrections, 10; descriptions, 21; longest, 40
Trailheads, 21
Tram Terminal, 27, 34, 41, 55, 58, 60. *See* Upper Tran Terminal
Tram Terminal service road, 55
Tramway Road, 28, 34, 37, 38
Tramway Trail, 34, 35; junction with La Luz, 30
Tree Spring Trail, 41, 46–47, 55
Tridents, 164–67
Tunnel Spring Trail, 42, 43–44
Turkey, 6
Turkey buzzard, 6
TWA Canyon, 168, 175, 176, 177
Tyrolean traverse, 116

U Mound, 195
UNM Spire, 27, 79, 94–97
U.S. Geological Survey Distribution Center, 10; maps, 9

USGS Sandia Crest topo map, error, 48, 49
Upper Domingo Baca Canyon, 167–92. *See Also* Domingo Baca Canyon
Upper Roadcut, 62

Vegetation, 3–5, 20, 51, 52
Vista Point, 135, 136
Viva la Revolución, 186, 188

Warpy Moople, 122, 126
Water, 13, 18–19, 21, 34, 38, 39, 41, 42, 43, 44, 45, 46, 47
Waterfall Canyon, 22, 24, 27; ice climbing, 25
Waterfall Canyon Trail, 22, 25
Waterstains, 136
Waterstains Route, 163
Weather, 3, 12, 13
West Chimney, 176
West Saddle, 132
Western Skies Motel, 195
Westeron Wynde, 172
White fir, 4
White Wash, 195
Wildcat, 181
Wildflowers, 4–5, 45
Wildlife checklist, 6. *See also Appendix*
Wildlife refuge, 6, 20
Willows, 4
Wind chill, 3. *See also* Equivalent chill temperature
Windy Ridge, 178
Winter: closure, 45; hiking, 17; temperature, 2